Living for

Exploring God's Interactive Plan of Hope

Elise Froelicher Olson

WESTBOW
PRESS®
A DIVISION OF THOMAS NELSON
& ZONDERVAN

Scripture taken from the Holy Bible, NEW INTERNATIONAL VERSION®. Copyright © 1973, 1978, 1984, 2011 by Biblica, Inc. All rights reserved worldwide. Used by permission. NEW INTERNATIONAL VERSION® and NIV® are registered trademarks of Biblica, Inc. Use of either trademark for the offering of goods or services requires the prior written consent of Biblica US, Inc.

Good News Translation® (Today's English Version, Second Edition) Copyright © 1992 American Bible Society. All rights reserved.

Scripture quotations taken from the Holy Bible, New Living Translation, Copyright © 1996, 2004. Used by permission of Tyndale House Publishers, Inc., Wheaton, Illinois 60189. All rights reserved.

Scripture taken from the Common English Bible®, CEB® Copyright © 2010, 2011 by Common English Bible.™ Used by permission. All rights reserved worldwide. The "CEB" and "Common English Bible" trademarks are registered in the United States Patent and Trademark Office by Common English Bible. Use of either trademark requires the permission of Common English Bible.

Some names have been changed within the true stories told in *Living for Love*.

WestBow Press books may be ordered through booksellers or by contacting:

WestBow Press
A Division of Thomas Nelson & Zondervan
1663 Liberty Drive
Bloomington, IN 47403
www.westbowpress.com
1 (866) 928-1240

ISBN: 978-1-5127-5226-7 (sc)
ISBN: 978-1-5127-5227-4 (hc)
ISBN: 978-1-5127-5225-0 (e)

Library of Congress Control Number: 2016913154

Print information available on the last page.

WestBow Press rev. date: 11/8/2016

Dedication

To my mother, Lorena Reid Embler,
my living example of Matthew 25:34–40.
"Then the King will say to those on his right,
'Come you are blessed by my Father;
Take your inheritance, the kingdom prepared
for you since the creation of the world.
For I was hungry and you gave me something to eat, I
was thirsty and you gave me something to drink,
I was a stranger and you invited me in, I
needed clothes and you clothed me,
I was sick and you looked after me, I was in
prison and you came to visit me.'
"Then the righteous will answer him, 'Lord, when
did we see you hungry and feed you,
or thirsty and give you something to drink? When
did we see you a stranger and invite you in,
or needing clothes and clothe you? When did we
see you sick and in prison and go to visit you?'
The King will reply, 'I tell you the truth,
whatever you did for one of the least of these
brothers of mine, you did for me.'"

The Great Commission

Then Jesus came to them and said,
"All authority in heaven and earth has been given to me.
Therefore go and make disciples of all nations, baptizing them
in the name of the Father and of the Son and of the Holy Spirit,
and teaching them to obey everything I have commanded you.
And surely I am with you always, to the very end of the age."
Matthew 28:18–20

Contents

Introduction

To be loved is wonderful! The warmth of knowing someone cares brightens our world. To love and be loved is our greatest gift and our greatest struggle. Most people agree that we should live by the golden rule, making time for the people around us and bringing hope to those who are less fortunate. No matter where we live or what our culture, the world would be a better place if people cared for each other, but in reality we each have our own agendas, desires, and demands that take so much of our time, energy, and resources. When we do set our minds to do something for someone, trying to make a difference can often be frustrating and elusive. To put someone else first is easier said than done. Yet, there are some people who consistently encourage others and have a loving way about them, though their lives may not be easy. What is their secret? How do they persevere with joy in a frustrating world?

Revealing the secrets to love found within the pages of the Bible is what this book, *Living for Love*, is all about. The loving God who created you and me and our beautiful, complex world, gave us a message. In sixty-six books, written by forty different authors from a wide variety of backgrounds, the Bible tells one true, cohesive story of God's great love for us. This relevant message teaches us about God's true character and helps us find true love. The Bible helps us to answer our questions and overcome our struggles as it guides us along the path of life, giving us hope. *Living for Love* explores God's interactive plan for our lives and was written in part for those who might consider the Bible outdated, overwhelming, or hard to follow. If your heart is open toward God and you would like an opportunity to discover what the pages reveal, let's go on the journey together.

God draws men and women through the beauty and complexity of nature and the love of others, giving us hope that God is real. Our hope and our needs motivate us to seek him, and when we do, we realize God knows us, loves us, and is there for us. Learning to love and to be loved the way God designed is the purpose of our life journey; it is what molds us and develops our character. We discover God's compassionate plan as we begin to trust his love and learn to follow his direction. God asks us to love him with all our heart, soul, mind, and strength and to love others as we love ourselves. This is the foundation for (and also summarizes) the Ten Commandments, our moral guidelines for living well (Matthew 22:37–40, Mark 12:30). Can we love God with all of our thoughts and emotions if we do not take the time to get to know him? How do we love people, showing as much concern for them as we do for ourselves when life is often overwhelming? We are so easily distracted, so busy, so easily hurt, so often tired, and so inwardly focused. How can we find the joy we are looking for in a frustrating world that often lures and deceives us with counterfeit comfort and love? God did not abandon us to live our life alone and handle life's difficulties without help. He longs to be active in our lives to guide, help, comfort, and teach us. In this book I have sought to summarize, in everyday language, the precepts taught in the Bible—how to live a life that is fulfilling, full of love, and that makes a difference for others. True stories illustrate how God interacts with everyday people. Questions at the end of each chapter help us apply God's message to our own lives and move us forward in our relationship with him and each other. Reading the book as a group will enhance understanding and build relationships as you share your thoughts and experiences. At the back of the book there are over 180 outreach ideas, listed alphabetically. The purpose of the list is to be a springboard to inspire your own God-given ideas and passions. My hope is that every reader will discover their part in God's vast, amazing, compassionate plan.

Once when I was telling some students about the many prophecies in the Bible (hundreds of details that were foretold and came true later in history) one Chinese young man said, "So, it is a fortune telling book!" I had never thought about it like that, although many historical events were foretold in the Bible with amazing detail, giving us evidence to affirm our faith. Yet the Bible is so much more; it is the living and active word of God that has the power to change lives! The Bible tells us how to secure our future—how we can be free of the things in our life that hold us back, how we can live for others, build strong relationships, find joy, and live forever. It tells us about the experiences of people before us and the faith, demonstrated by action, which defined their success. The message is a story of hope; God's grace and love is available to everyone! God longs for us to become part of his family and to prepare us to enter a new world—a wonderful eternal world we cannot even fully imagine; a world where there is no more heartache, death, crying, or pain and where love is real and ever present. Will you listen to his quiet voice calling out to you? Do you want to follow him? Will you tell God that you need him?

CHAPTER 1

Hope

Hope hears the whisper of the wind,
And grows within our hearts.
A song bird's gentle, joyful tune,
Who calls, "Please come take part."

Yesterday, I saw a hummingbird at sunset. The speedy, whimsical little bird hovered as if to say hello, its iridescent feathers silhouetted against the gold and orange sky painted above the Pacific. Then it began to dance, flitting back and forth in time, its slender beak moving as if conducting an angelic orchestra. The colorful hummingbird gave me a feeling of joy. Such unexpected beauty filled my soul—a creative message of a reality beyond what I could see—hope!

The beauty and creativity in nature is one way God reaches out to humanity with hope. From star-filled galaxies to the aquatic communities of the coral reefs, the natural world has complexity, variety, color, and splendor beyond our wildest imaginations. Consider the peacock—quite an extraordinary bird! Did the peacock originate from a random process? Or did someone imagine beforehand his ornate feathers, topped with the colorful green and blue medallion design that fans out behind him as he struts? The detail and beauty of our natural world give us a measure of evidence that God exists. He demonstrates his majesty and power, yet he calls to us individually with surprises in nature, such as my encounter with a wonderful little hummingbird or my friend's birthday snow, though unlikely, falling year after year on her day, for her delight! God is calling out to us through his creation, "Don't miss the life I desire for you, a life of purpose and hope. I will teach you, if you are willing. Do you trust me?"*

We are humbled and delighted by the beauty and power of nature, sparking within us the mixed emotions of wonder, fear, and hope. Our world is amazingly creative and complex, with dynamic change and remarkable energy and life, even beyond that which we can see. Could we reason then, there is also a plan for humankind—God's cherished, created in his image (Genesis 1:26–28)? If God has created each one of us, unique within a sea of diversity, does he also care about and have a purpose for each of us? Does he have a purpose for humankind as a whole and is it possible that part of his purpose is to love us and receive our love in return? Is his intention to demonstrate just how dynamic and invincible real love is? God is set on reaching out to all humanity with his love (John 3:16, 2 Peter 3:9) and his "hope" is to use us (Matthew 28:19, 20)! His plan from the beginning is that we would care for this earth and one another (Genesis 1 and 2), yet history has shown that without his intervention and help we have a hard time taking care of anything. Still, he has not given up on us, but poured out everything in order for us to learn about true love. God's interactive plan is both beautiful and ingenious, because as we receive his love we are also empowered to love others. With his help, moment by moment, day by day, we learn to be the people he desires for us to become, tuning in to the world around us with a thankful heart. We need God's help to see with his eyes, to listen and really hear, and to discover what is important and what role he has planned for us.

We are all looking for acceptance and security. Everyone needs love and encouragement: you, your family and friends, those in authority, the people you work with, and the cashier where you do business—everybody! Will we look beyond our own needs to see the hearts and needs of others? Life in our world is often hard and unfair, yet it can also be full of goodness and joy. Sharing our lives—our time, a smile, words of encouragement, help in times of trouble—makes a difference. Encouragement is a gift that can soothe a hurt, uphold a dream, or even inspire someone to live the life God intended for them. Our gentle kindness gives rise to a lasting hope that cannot disappoint—the truth that the God of the universe loves us! "And we rejoice in the hope of the glory of God. Not only so, but we also rejoice in our suffering, because we know that suffering produces perseverance; perseverance, character; and character, hope. And hope does not disappoint us, because God has poured out his love into our hearts by the Holy Spirit, whom he has given us" (Romans 5:2b–5). God is telling us that our character, if rooted in the love of God and developed by life's trials, will have a positive effect and in the long run we will not be disappointed. Despite life's hardships, there is a God who sees us and who loves us. As we learn to love from God himself, our lives become a reflection of the glory of God. A mother with hungry children can look into the eyes of a humanitarian and see hope and life. A young man, struggling to provide for his family, feels the hand of God on him when someone provides him with a job that does not compromise what is right. A little child feels God's love when a tired parent, at the end of their rope, looks at them and says, "I love you."

To have a life of satisfaction and joy we need to learn to love. It sounds easy, almost natural, but within our relationships we soon realize it is not easy; perhaps that is part of the plan too. It is hard to put our wants and needs aside for the sake of someone else. It is hard to hear others when no one is listening to us. It is hard to relinquish our plan to commit to someone else's, even if it is God's plan. We cannot do it on our own and as conflicts arise in our relationships, we long for comfort and help. If we turn to God, he promises to give us the love and the help we need. Everyone needs the grace of others, which starts with the grace of God. His desire is to pour his grace and love out into our lives; if we are willing to accept it, that love overflows. We become a source of hope, reflecting God's character, even learning to love at "unlovable moments," and imparting grace to a world in need. Will we pour indifference, impatience, and anger out on our world, or will we hear God's call and learn to love? Will we listen to his call and respond? Even when we are not sure of God's direction—*"Is this God's whisper?"* If we sense God directing us, will we take action? Test by asking, *"Is this action loving and good? Is God asking me to make a change in my life that will improve my relationships?"* If so, do it! *Do* the good thing you think you are sensing, whether it is God's idea or yours. God longs to demonstrate compassion and reveal his reality in and through your life. Day by day he is faithful to show us the way—to help us, correct us, mature us, and most of all, love us!

Responding to God's prompting is an important step in learning to love. Extraordinarily, responding also sets us free to love as we begin to overcome our fears and as God blesses our willingness. Listening and acting upon what we know or even sense God wants from us demonstrates our love for God (John 14:15). We grow in experiencing what true love is as we are rooted in God's love and we will more naturally move in it, touching the lives of others. God's loving nature starts to become part of our nature! As we experience the joy of putting a ray of hope and happiness in someone's life it motivates us. We realize that the risk and sacrifice is worth it. And that is not the end; the hope we give others has the potential to bring them to God, who is the very source of love and hope. In turn he enables them to act and do good for others who are trying to find their way. Like a pebble on the water God's love has a ripple effect, first within our own hearts and then radiating out to our community and our world.

There are countless ways to encourage hope—inspiring people to have courage and confidence. We can encourage someone with something as simple as a touch or as elaborate as creating an organization to meet basic needs, such as clean drinking water or food. We can encourage someone as close as our spouse or someone we have never met, halfway around the world. We can encourage others by listening, helping, giving, praying, teaching, and working beside them. God has made us each unique and placed us within a time and community to touch the lives of others in our unique way. "For we are God's workmanship, created in Jesus Christ to do good works, which God prepared in advance for us to do" (Ephesians 2:10). It is God's plan that we become his ambassadors—his light in the darkness. Our love shown to others is a stepping stone in the path to believing God is real; faith grows within ourselves as we learn to trust him and hope rises within others as they experience our kindness. With purpose, he has chosen *us* to reveal his love and life to the world.

5

God Created the Flowers—We Give them Away!

Alone, overwhelmed, and stressed out, Jenny wondered how she would have the strength to continue on day after day with so many demands. Working to pay the bills and caring for her children as a single parent was taking a toll on her; if it weren't for the children, she would be tempted to give up. She often felt she was letting them down. One day as she arrived home, a neighbor invited her and her boys to come to dinner. At first she hesitated, feeling awkward and worried about how the boys would behave. Realizing she had not even had time to think about what they were going to eat that evening, she gratefully accepted. She began to relax at the table as they engaged her children with stories and questions. She had learned to trust her neighbors over the last few months, so before leaving she gave them an extra key in case of an emergency. The next day when she returned home, she found the couple had stocked her refrigerator, picked up her apartment and even set fresh flowers on her table. Their practical love gave her hope. Each time she gazed at the colorful flowers that week, she smiled and found renewed strength. Maybe someone really did care and maybe she was not alone after all!

Flowers brighten our world, whether the color of a flower market bringing life to a gray city street or a dozen roses given to proclaim a man's love. With their array of colors, delicate petals, and sweet fragrances, they hold a special place in nature as they declare spring and bring hope and delight. One of my mother's greatest joys was flowers, but it still took us by surprise when she decided to start a dahlia farm. She explained they would have to dig up the bulbs each fall and plant them again in the spring. I remember my response,

"Mom! That sounds like a lot of work for you and dad. How much money can you make on dahlias? Can't you pick an easier flower?" She planted a huge field of dahlias and opened *Lorena's Dahlia Farm.* It was beautiful. She cultivated the flowers, cut and gathered them, and delivered them to local florists. I am not sure how much money she made, because she gave them away as often as she sold them. She gave them to friends and family, to the sick, to people who were alone, or anyone else she felt could use a visit and a cheerful bouquet. She even gave flowers to the blind; after all, her blind friends loved the smell. That's my mom!

Gardens full of flowers and fields of food are a beautiful illustration of how God designed our world. God created flowers, plants, bushes, and trees, with all their varieties and fragrances, and with their beautiful array of colors, shapes, and fruits, reflecting his world the way it was meant to be. God provides his blessings of life-giving seeds and bulbs, fertile soil, and rain, yet a garden or field needs our care and cultivation to reach its full potential. Cultivation takes effort—our time, toil, and creativity, yet without God's miracle of growth it is for nothing. God and man working together bring about the most remarkable beauty and bounty. The role of a hummingbird is another garden example of God's relationship with us. A plant cannot produce seed or fruit without pollination. The wind on its own can blow the pollen from one flower or plant to another, pollinating to produce fruit and seed for the next generation, but more often the hummingbirds or the bees carry the pollen from one to another; it is their food. Likewise, God can work on his own to carry his plan to the next generation, but in his design he uses us. The living Spirit of truth transfers life from one believer to another by the "pollen" of God's grace and love, and by that love we are nourished. We take part in God's plan as we share our lives with others, just as the little hummingbird plays a role by pollinating the continued splendor of a garden.

As a garden blooms or a field matures, if we never gather the colorful flowers or harvest the crops for others, most people will not have the opportunity to see the beauty, smell the sweet fragrance, eat the fresh foods, or experience the joy they bring. In the same way God has entrusted us to care for this world and share our growing love and blessings with others. He longs for us to do the satisfying work of cultivating our relationships with him and those closest to us. Then as beautiful love grows within our garden of family and friends, God beckons us to give love away to others outside the garden.

The Bible is often called God's love letter to humankind because it tells us about God's overriding love for the people he created and how he has made it possible for us to be a loving force in our world. His plan for us is interactive, so talk to God about your life. Ask God to answer your questions, to give you direction, to calm your fears, and to heal your hurts. Ask him to help you to trust him each day. Tell him what would encourage you. Ask God how you could encourage someone else. Listen to his correction and call. If you feel something stopping you, ask God to help you move forward. Admit to him any changes you need to make. By writing your thoughts and recording what happens over time, you will be able to see more clearly God's intervention and provision, as well as how he is using you. As you learn to listen and respond to God's direction, you will experience the joy of beginning to know God in a personal way. In the chapters that follow, let's learn more of what the Bible teaches us about God's compassionate and interactive plan to restore our lives and our world. There is hope!

> And so we know and rely on the love God has for us. God is Love. Whoever lives in love, lives in God and God in them. 1 John 4:16

> And God is able to bless you abundantly, so that in all things at all times, having all that you need, you will abound in every good work. 2 Corinthians 9:8

> Again Jesus said, "Peace be with you! As the Father has sent me, I am sending you." John 20:21

> We are therefore Christ's ambassadors, as though God were making his appeal through us. 2 Corinthians 5:20a

> "You are the light of the world... let your light shine before others, that they may see your good deeds and glorify your Father in heaven." Matthew 5:14-16

> Therefore encourage one another and build each other up, ... 1 Thessalonians 5:11a

> Your love has given me much joy and comfort, my brother, for your kindness has often refreshed the hearts of God's people. Philemon 1:7 (NTL)

*Romans 1:20, Jeremiah 29:11–13, Psalm 25:1–14, Proverbs 3:5–6

Group Discussion:

Answer the questions to which you relate, being honest to your experience. Participation is always voluntary.

1. Have you ever experienced a time when seeing and/or feeling the wonder and beauty of nature gave you a sense of peace or joy? Share your experience. Do you have a picture to share?
2. Share about a time when someone's encouragement made a difference in your life. Was it something big or small and how did it make a difference?
3. Do you believe there are things God planned for you to do before you were even born? Why or why not?
4. Is it possible for us to turn away from God's "hope" for us and do what we want to do instead?
5. What stops you from reaching out to someone on your mind—your family, your friend, your co-worker? Could it be that God is placing this person on your heart for a purpose?
6. What might stop *you* from receiving the love of others?
7. Share a time when you experienced God shining his light into a dark situation for you.

CHAPTER 2

Spirit of Truth

Is truth playing hide and seek with me?
The One who made me, knows me.
God sees all angles of reality,
He loves truth, do I?
He loves, can I?

We are all longing for the truth! The truth brings freedom and opens our hearts to God's love and message of hope. We are all longing for direction and God is longing for us to seek him so that he can show us the way. Ultimately, we are all looking for the same thing—true love! Yet, there is a world of lies seducing us from the truth and lies never lead us to true love. How can we find what our hearts desire? "If you love me, keep my commands. And I will ask the Father, and he will give you another advocate to help you and be with you forever—the Spirit of truth" (John 14:15–17a). God promises he will not leave us as orphans, but will live with us and show us the way. We are more vulnerable to the deception in this world than we realize. To find truth, direction, and loving relationships we need to walk the path of life with the Holy Spirit of truth.

It is valuable to know the truth. Before Jesus, not everyone had access to the truth because of humankind's separation from God. Some people try to do the right thing, while others don't really care. Some people fool themselves, convincing themselves the wrong they are doing is right. Others seek to deceive and destroy. No matter which categories we fall into, we are all separated from God because of our selfish nature. God is the very source and essence of good and truth, and though he draws us, we shrink back and disengage because of our lack of love and our guilt. This separation even leads many to believe there is no God. God gave us this world to take care of, but we have made a mess of it, just as we often make a mess of our relationships with our family, our friends, and our neighbors. Ultimately, we hurt ourselves. Deceptive thoughts from within and the lies of the world around us keep us lost and alone, feeding the chaos of our lives. We need a trusting relationship with the God who created us to be a part of his plan to redeem our lives and our world, yet we are separated from him. Do you feel it?

Our separation from God is a big problem and Jesus came to solve it! He came in a most unexpected way—as a baby—his human mother, a young virgin girl named Mary, and his Father the Spirit of God (Luke 1:26–38). He is both the Son of God and the Son of Man, which he often called himself. Jesus, who always was, came from heaven to earth to give us the help we so desperately needed. As God, Jesus' perfection enabled him to live as a man without ever doing wrong. Therefore, as man, he could pay for humanity's sin as a perfect Messiah (Savior), something we could never do for ourselves. No matter where you are from or what your religion,

Jesus came to provide peace with God for you. Jesus willingly suffered and died on a cross to take the punishment for the whole world's sin! He broke the ultimate power of sin and death in our lives and rose again to life after three days. Jesus upheld justice by paying sin's penalty and fulfilled God's promise of hope, setting us free! He endured it all for the *joy* (Hebrews 12:2) of seeing us reconciled to Father God and the *joy* of seeing his children reach out to one another in love—the joy of providing us a way home. Now, if we acknowledge this great gift, and accept it for ourselves, we can have a close relationship with God. Namely, the Holy Spirit of truth can reside within us! The death and resurrection of Jesus brought about the time in history when God can direct our lives in a very personal way to accomplish his compassionate plan. In Old Testament times (before Jesus came) only special people had access to God's Spirit, the Spirit of truth. Now, since the arrival of the Spirit of truth recorded in the book of Acts, everyone has the opportunity to be directed by the same Spirit as Moses, Elijah, or David. As with them, we need to cooperate with him, so that God can work with us and through us as we learn to love.

So how do we cooperate with the Spirit of truth? God knows each of us better than we know ourselves. He wants us to know him through a loving relationship, now possible because Jesus bridged the separation (caused by sin) that kept us apart. If we willingly accept the amazing gift of what Jesus has done for us, we can have the Holy Spirit living with us, giving us comfort, confidence, and determination guided by love. "For the Spirit God gave us does not make us timid, but gives us power, love, and self-discipline" (2 Timothy 1:7). We cannot see the Holy Spirit of truth, but we can get to know him as we trust him day by day. We cooperate as we seek

God in the situations of our lives and in his word, letting him help us—learning his ways, listening, and most importantly, obeying (Matthew 7:7–12). He wants to give us good gifts, teaching us to love. Jesus was our example; when he walked on this earth he relied entirely on the Father. He said "Very truly I tell you, the Son can do nothing by himself; he can do only what he sees his Father doing, because whatever the Father does the Son also does" (John 5:19). The Spirit of truth helps us to see what God is doing. As we desire to know and follow God, the Spirit of truth guides and helps us to do his will. Everybody wants their life to make a difference and to be a part of something lasting and good. Jesus said in John 15:5, "... apart from me you can do nothing." Jesus showed us that he relies on his relationship with the Father and we need to rely on Jesus and the Spirit of truth, who are our connection to the Father as well.

Some readers may find it confusing when we talk about the Father God, Jesus (Son of God, Son of Man), and the Holy Spirit of truth, so let's take a moment to clarify. There is **one** holy, perfect, good, all knowing, powerful, and loving God (Deuteronomy 6:4, Mark 12:29, Galatians 3:20). To accomplish his purposes, God reveals himself as three persons (Matthew 28:19, 1 Peter 1:1–2) and God can do this all at the same time. The roles of our triune God cannot be entirely separated, but to help us grasp the concept we can make some distinctions. Our Father God is reigning over all the earth with goodness, wisdom, and power (Psalms 147:1–11, 89:4–6). Jesus, his only Son, came to earth to teach us, to show us God's character (John 10:30), to be our example, and to save us from our selfishness and sin (John 3:16–17). Jesus came to end the separation we had with God and he now intercedes for us (Romans 8:34–38). Jesus will eventually judge us (John 5:22). The Holy Spirit of truth guides us to conviction and truth, providing us comfort and healing as he dwells within us. He directs us daily as we allow him. (John 14:16–18, Romans 8:1–28) In unity, God created the universe and you and me (Did you know plural pronouns are used for God throughout the creation account, found in the book of Genesis?). God the Father, Jesus, and the Spirit of truth are one, entirely, as 1x1x1=1. Perfect unity in character and mission may help to explain part of the complexity of *one God* revealed in three persons. It may be hard for us to absorb, but don't let that get in the way of your belief. Consider all the mysteries of nature and our advanced technological world that we find difficult to understand. God's thoughts, intellect, and plans are infinitely beyond ours (Isaiah 55:9)! How then can mere men understand the whole of our majestic God? Yet through God's word, and also our experience, he teaches us he is the Father, Son, and Holy Spirit, (the Trinity) the <u>one true God</u>.

Prayer—talking and listening to God—is essential for the Spirit of truth to be active in our lives as we develop our relationship with him. Prayer is how we gain understanding and instruction, along with reading the Bible and meeting with other believers. We ask for forgiveness, receive comfort, express thankfulness, and find our place in his plan as we are guided by the Spirit of truth. Our hopes are realized and power is unleashed for good in this world as we call upon God in prayer and trust his guidance and activity. We learn to respond to his "still small voice" as we sense and confirm the direction he gives us. God's direction will never be contrary to the precepts of his word, the Bible. It is a practical matter, because we do not have the inside story, but God does and will help us see more clearly as we respond to what he shows us. We may not recognize a lack of love in our own hearts, but God can gently correct us, and as we become willing to change he gives us his peace. We do not know the hearts of those around us, their lives, emotions, thoughts, hurts, or motives. We can only observe clues, but God knows fully what it is happening around us, so we can trust him for guidance to take actions that will help. Prayer is practical and necessary in order to change within and also to reach out in a way that affects the truth of the situation. As we rely on the Spirit of truth we grow in our relationship with God and he helps us to understand truth and to act in love.

God invites us to join him in his plan for our world. As we are seeking to know God and partner with him, he will test us with small things at first and with actions of greater consequence as we listen and respond. God helps us to be authentic, caring, and wise as we learn how to reach out to others effectively. What a feeling of joy when we find ourselves right in the middle of God's plan. There will be times when the intensity of being used by God in a dark world leaves us clinging to him for new strength and wisdom. Clinging to God, relying on him is where the power is found. Lives are changed, both our own and others, as we rely on the Spirit of truth. God is here, wanting to help us, wanting to give us direction and purpose, but we must desire it enough to give up our control and allow him access to our lives. We learn to trust him, day by day, moment by moment. Will we follow God's guidance for our lives? Will we get involved in the lives of others when he prompts us or turn the other way? We can trust God to be with us if we are willing to step forward. Allowing God to change us, to move us, and to help us as we reach out with patience and love is evidence that our faith is real!

Jesus came so that we could be set free from the lies that deceive us and pull us down. We now have the Spirit of truth to help us call upon God's love each day. God asks us to join him in his mission of love for our world and enables us step by step as we go forward. Evil is constantly trying to get us to doubt the word of God—just like in the book of Genesis when the serpent questioned Eve, "Did God really say...?" (Genesis 3). If we react based on lies that plant doubt, rather than the truth of God's love, we are on a dangerous course, vulnerable, insecure, and defensive. Turning to God and trusting his plan gives us reliable help to find truth and a life of love as we join God in his work. We *need* the Spirit of truth!

> The true light that gives light to everyone has come into the world. John 1:9

> "If you love me, keep my commands and I will ask the Father, and he will give you another advocate to help you and be with you forever—the Spirit of truth. The world cannot accept him, because it neither sees him nor knows him. But you know him, for he lives with you and will be in you. I will not leave you as orphans; I will come to you. Before long, the world will not see me anymore, but you will see me. Because I live, you also will live. On that day you will realize that I am in my Father, and you are in me, and I am in you." John 14:15–20

> "But when he, the Spirit of truth, comes, he will guide you into all the truth. He will not speak on his own; he will speak only what he hears, and he will tell you what is yet to come. He will glorify me because it is from me that he will receive what he will make known to you." John 16:13–14

Dear friends, since God so loved us, we ought to love one another. No one has ever seen God; but if we love one another, God lives in us and his love is made complete in us. This is how we know that we live in him and he in us: He has given us his Spirit. And we have seen and testify that the Father has sent the Son to be the Savior of the world. If anyone acknowledges that Jesus is the Son of God, God lives in them and they in God. And so we know and rely on the love God has for us. God is love. Whoever lives in love lives in God, and God in them. This is how love is made complete among us so that we will have confidence on the Day of Judgment: In this world we are like Jesus. 1 John 4:11–17

Surely you desire truth in the inner parts; you teach me wisdom in the inmost place. Psalm 51:6 (NIV © 1965)

GOD, I need you, help me! I need the Spirit of truth in order to hear and see as you do, and to act as you would.

She Listened!

Mavis lives on the steep, birch-lined bank of Long Lake in northern Minnesota. One morning, as she looked out at the lake, she felt God "nudging" her thoughts that neighbors nearby needed her. They were an elderly couple, the man in his eighties. His wife, who suffered from kidney failure, was in a hospital in Fargo, North Dakota—three hours away, but Mavis did not know this. She picked up the phone and called to discover that he was sobbing. He longed to be with his wife, but could not drive. Though Mavis herself was in her seventies, she often drove to Fargo to visit family. She told him to pack a bag and she would be right there to take him to the hospital. What a joy and relief that he could be by his sick wife's side. His visit lifted his wife's spirit and she soon got well enough to come home for a time. He has called Mavis his angel since then. She listened to God's still voice and had taken action!

Why Didn't I Listen?

As a youth I had the nickname *Elsie the Cow* from my commonly mispronounced name connected with an old, but at the time popular, advertisement for Borden Milk. Like many teens I went through a very awkward stage—thick glasses, braces, and my nickname didn't help! I was often "mooed" at and made fun of. Being in my own little world most of the time, it did not bother me as much as it might have, but when it came to boys I felt very unattractive. In my sophomore year of high school a boy on the football team asked me out. I was awestruck! I believed I would follow God's rules when it came to dating. I believed in remaining sexually pure until marriage, but as the months passed I was put to the test. I began to *think* if I wanted to keep my boyfriend I needed to make him happy by having sex. I would say to myself, "*If I don't, he will be disappointed, perhaps even angry and I may lose him. Anyway, he gave me a beautiful promise ring. He loves me; we will be together forever! What difference does it really make? I am not hurting anyone.*" How easily I allowed my thoughts to deceive me! Why is it, so often, only by experience do we finally understand that God's rules are for our protection and future happiness? We did not end up together, but rather he soon found someone else that he wanted to be with.

The Holy Spirit of truth was calling out to me, but I pushed away his warning in exchange for counterfeit love. Listening would have prevented the pain and disappointment. God was trying to protect me. I found myself lost in the time that followed, as I made decisions based on my own opinion or the world's changing views of what is right. I felt alone and I needed the Holy Spirit to guide me, yet I was the one getting in the way of our relationship, closing my ears, and not admitting how selfish and disobedient I had become. I wanted to be loved, but I was cutting myself off from true love. Eventually I started to listen to the Spirit of truth and I turned and sought after God and his plan for me. He helped me, day by day, to have a life worth living. Where would I be without the Spirit of truth?

Group Discussion:

1. Share an example of when you made a choice or reacted based on something that was not true.
2. Do you believe God knows the whole truth? If so, do you find this scary, comforting, or both?
3. Have you experienced a time in your life that you felt God was trying to warn you *not* to do something? Did you listen? Explain if you are willing. (If you did it anyway, find comfort in Romans 8:28.)
4. Do you believe the Spirit of truth is available to help us individually? Give an example.
5. How did Jesus make our relationship with the Spirit of truth possible?
6. Read Matthew 13:1–23. Why do you think Jesus said that people with healthy eyes and ears could not see or hear? The people who gathered to hear Jesus did not yet have the Spirit of truth to help them. In the explanation of the parable of the sower what keeps us from being fruitful and how can the Spirit of truth help us?
7. Have you ever felt the Holy Spirit prompt you to do something for someone else? What happened?
8. Have you ever obeyed God in a small thing that led to knowing more about a bigger plan God had for your life? Explain.

CHAPTER 3

True Love

The twinkle of the stars, the sparkle of the light upon
the water, the elusive colors of the rainbow—
Reflected light calling us to true love.
We are the light of the world, the warmth of our God.

God is love. (From 1 John 4:16)

Everyone is looking for true love, a love that will make us feel secure and valued. Yet our idea of what true love looks like is usually flawed. The fairy-tale idea of happily ever after in this present fallen world often brings disappointment. True love starts with God's love for us and our realization of that great love. To love and to be loved the way God desires us to, whether within our marriages or our relationships with family, friends, and neighbors, is impossible to sustain without God's help. As we yield our lives to the Spirit of truth, who is love in person, God's love comforts us and flows through us to others. This kind of love takes people by surprise! *How wonderful that someone is taking a genuine interest in me. How unexpected when someone shows love to me when I have hurt them.* If we could begin to love our enemies, that love would break down misconceptions and offer peace. Giving ourselves to love like this is something we cannot do effectively unless we connect with God; he is the source of true love. Receiving genuine love helps us to take down our walls, and as we do a glimmer of hope arises—perhaps happiness is possible. God is calling out to each of us because he loves us beyond measure! God is pursuing us with passion; he truly wants to teach us to trust him and to learn to love. Discovering and experiencing God's love is the pathway to finding eternal love—love that gives us the warmth, security, and value we are looking for in our relationship with God and each other. *True love exists after all!*

True love starts with God's passionate love for us! Think back to a moment in life when you felt deep love for someone—perhaps your wedding day, gazing at a newborn child, or for someone who gave you an incredible gift. Or perhaps you can remember a time when you felt loved through and through. Even if you have never felt an overwhelming love, imagine love that deep, and then know it is but a shadow of the amazing love God has for you! There is nothing we need to do to be loved by God and there is nothing we can do, anyone can do, to separate us from his love. "For I am convinced that neither death nor life, neither angels nor demons, neither the present or the future, nor any powers, neither height nor depth, nor anything else in all creation will be able to separate us from the love of God that is in Christ Jesus our Lord" (Romans 8:38–39). Take a moment to let this great truth sink in! The source of true love is God himself and he longs to pour out his love into our lives and then through our lives. Our relationship with him is voluntary, or it could not be love, but whatever our response to God's love, his love remains true.

God knows our insecure nature, how we put up walls, how we often hide from him and each other, so he pursues us. "For God so loved the world that he gave his one and only Son, that whoever believes in him shall not perish but have eternal life. For God did not send his Son into the world to condemn the world, but to save the world through him" (John 3:16–17). This is passionate love— God allowing his only Son to live and die as man for the purpose of pursuing us! God prepares a loving home for us (John 14:2) and saves us from all the sin and lies that lure us away from it. Jesus was willing to leave the perfection of heaven and die at our hands, though he is all powerful, so that we could receive the Spirit of truth. The living God of the universe can now be *with us* to comfort and empower us by his love. Jesus' sacrificial love defeated the power of sin and death for us all, so we can experience true love—a love that never dies. We no longer need to be afraid to go into his light, no matter what our past is. He calls us to turn away from the darkness and receive his amazing love. If we are willing to trust him, God's great love tears down the walls that keep us apart. His promise is to ultimately bring us to a place of perfect love. In the meantime God is teaching us about true love and how to reach out to a world that needs him desperately. Learning to reflect God's love is an essential part of God's plan. If we cannot love, how could God's promise of a place of perfect love in eternity become reality? Here in our present world our love will never be perfect, but as we allow God's love to flow through us we learn to love and as we pass into eternal life, God promises to complete in us the gift of perfect love (Philippians 1:6–11).

"Love is patient, love is kind. It does not envy, it does not boast, it is not proud. It does not dishonor others, it is not self-seeking, it is not easily angered, it keeps no record of wrongs. Love does not delight in evil, but rejoices in the truth. It always protects, always trusts, always hopes, always perseveres. Love never fails" (1 Corinthians 13:4–8a). Wow, it would be wonderful to be loved like this! If our marriages reflected this definition of love we would all live happily ever after. I don't know about you, but I fall short. The truth is that God cannot use us to show his love without residing with us, and he cannot reside with us without something being done about our selfish and self-reliant state! I see my need for Jesus and for the Spirit of truth to guide me moment by moment. The whole of the Old Testament shows that we could not become people of righteousness, which means people of love, on our own, no matter how we tried. The same is true today, but *now* we have God's help to act in true love—a sacrificial love. To know the joy of this kind of love is satisfying. It is a wonderful, eternal joy! This kind of love has wonderful, eternal results—"love never fails!" (Corinthians 13:8a).

One of the keys to true love is forgiveness. The Parable of the Unmerciful Servant in Matthew 18 echoes Jesus' teaching in the Lord's Prayer: "Forgive us our debts, as we also have forgiven our debtors...For if you forgive other people when they sin against you, your heavenly Father will also forgive you. But if you do not forgive sins, your Father will not forgive your sin" (Matthew 6:12, 14–15). God has complete confidence in his love enabling us to forgive others if we are willing to embrace it. Even our prayers are affected if we harbor unforgiveness in our hearts (Mark 11:25). God forgave and will forgive us so much; he asks us to reflect his character by doing the same. Forgiveness in our relationships can start even before the offender is sorry and the relationship is fully restored. We free ourselves by forgiving within our hearts and loving others just the way they are. Full restoration and healing in relationships come when those who have done harm are truly sorry, ask forgiveness, and back it up with loving action. The grace we show toward others, within healthy boundaries, can help bring them to truly regret the hurt they have caused and to seek God for the help to change. Showing our love and grace in the process is what it means to be like Jesus. It is true love!

God loves us and wants our love in return; from this two-way love all that is good can flow out into our world. Let's take a look at God's call to love in the Bible.

Old Testament:

> "Hear, O Israel: The Lord our God, the Lord is one. Love the Lord your God with all your heart and with all your soul and with all your strength. These commands that I give to you today are to be upon your hearts. Impress them on your children. Talk about them when you sit at home and when you walk along the road, when you lie down and when you get up." Deuteronomy 6:4–7

> "Do not seek revenge or bear a grudge against anyone among your people, but love your neighbor as yourself. I am the Lord." Leviticus 19:18

For the Lord your God is God of gods and Lord of lords, the great God, mighty and awesome, God who shows no partiality and accepts no bribes. He defends the cause of the fatherless and the widow, and he loves the foreigner residing among you, giving them food and clothing. And you are to love foreigners... Deuteronomy 10:17–19a

Hatred stirs up conflict, but love covers over all wrong. Proverbs 10:12

Give thanks to the Lord, for he is good; his love endures forever. Psalm 107:1

What a man desires is unfailing love... Proverbs 19:22a

New Testament:

"Teacher, which is the greatest commandment in the law?" Jesus replied: "'Love the Lord your God with all your heart and with all your soul and with all your mind.' This is the first and greatest commandment. And the second is like it: 'Love your neighbor as yourself.' All the Law and Prophets hang on these two commandments." Matthew 22:36–40

"Of all of the commandments, which is the most important?" "The most important one," answered Jesus, "is this: 'Hear, O Israel: The Lord our God, the Lord is one. Love the Lord your God with all your heart and with all your soul and with all your mind and with all your strength.' The second is this:

'Love your neighbor as yourself.' There is no commandment greater than these." Mark 12:28b–31

Jesus answered the question of who our neighbor is by telling a story. He helps us to look at the question from a different perspective in The Parable of the Good Samaritan recorded in Luke 10:25–37:

On one occasion an expert in the law stood up to test Jesus. "Teacher," he asked, "what must I do to inherit eternal life?"

"What is written in the Law?" he replied. "How do you read it?"

He answered: "'Love the Lord your God with all your heart and with all your soul and with all your strength and with all your mind'; and, 'Love your neighbor as yourself.'"

"You have answered correctly," Jesus replied. "Do this and you will live."

But he wanted to justify himself, so he asked Jesus, "And who is my neighbor?"

In reply Jesus said: "A man was going down from Jerusalem to Jericho, when he was attacked by robbers. They stripped him of his clothes, beat him and went away, leaving him half dead. A priest happened to be going down the same road, and when he saw him, passed by on the other side. So too, a Levite, when he came to the place and saw him, passed by on the other side. But a Samaritan, as he traveled, came where the man was; and when he saw him, he took pity on him. He went to him and bandaged his wounds, pouring on oil and wine. Then he put the man on his own donkey, brought him to an inn and took care of him. The next day he took out two denarii and gave them to the innkeeper. 'Look after him,' he said, 'and when I return, I will reimburse you for any extra expense you may have.'

"Which of these three do you think was a neighbor to the man who fell into the hands of robbers?"

The expert in the law replied, "The one who had mercy on him."

Jesus told him, "Go and do likewise." Luke 10:25–37

We learn that in God's eyes to be a neighbor is to care for others, even if we do not know them or if they are not like us. Anyone in our path qualifies as our neighbor. We see that the Good Samaritan went the extra mile, doing far beyond what might be expected. We begin to get a sense that caring like this is beyond us, without God's help. But Jesus does not stop there!

"You have heard that it was said, 'Love your neighbor and hate your enemy.' But I tell you, love your enemies and pray for those who persecute you, that you might be children of your Father in heaven." Matthew 5:43–45a

"If you love those who love you, what credit is that to you? Even sinners love those who love them. And if you do good to those who are good to you, what credit is that to you? Even sinners do that. And if you lend to those from whom you expect repayment, what credit is that to you? Even sinners lend to sinners, expecting to be repaid in full. But love your enemies, do good to them, and lend to them without expecting to get anything back. Then your reward will be great, and you will be children of the Most High, because he is kind to the ungrateful and wicked. Be merciful, just as your Father is merciful." Luke 6:32–36

"A new command I give you: Love one another. As I have loved you, so you must love one another. By this everyone will know that you are my disciples, if you love one another." John 13:34–35

Did you know at the time Jesus told the Parable of the Good Samaritan that the Samaritans considered the Levites their enemies?

Be devoted to one another in love. Honor one another above yourselves. Romans 12:10

"As the Father has loved me, so have I loved you. Now remain in my love. If you keep my commands, you will remain in my love, just as I have kept my Father's commands and remain in his love. I have told you this so that my joy may be in you and that your joy may be complete. My command is this:

Love each other as I have loved you. Greater love has no one than this: to lay down one's life for one's friends. You are my friends if you do what I command." John 15:9–14.

Jesus is saying he loves us as much as the Father loves him! Let that first sentence sink in! He also says we have the opportunity to be his friends!

Dear friends, let us love one another, for love comes from God. Everyone who loves has been born of God and knows God. Whoever does not love does not know God, because **God is love**. This is how God showed his love among us: He sent his one and only Son into the world that we might live through him. This is love: not that we loved God, but that he loved us and sent his Son as an atoning sacrifice for our sins. Dear friends, since God so loved us, we also ought to love one another. No one has ever seen God; but if we love one another, God lives in us and his love is made complete in us. 1 John 4:7–12

But the fruit of the Spirit is love, joy, peace, forbearance, kindness, goodness, faithfulness, gentleness and self-control. Against such things there is no law. Galatians 5:22–23

Above all, love each other deeply, because love covers over a multitude of sins. Offer hospitality to one another without grumbling. 1 Peter 4:8–9

Whoever claims to love God yet hates his brother or sister is a liar. For whoever does not love their brother and sister, whom they have seen, cannot love God, whom they have not seen. 1 John 4:20

See what great love the Father has lavished on us, that we should be called the children of God! And that is what we are! ... Everyone who sins breaks the law; in fact sin is lawlessness. But you know that he appeared so that he might take away our sins. And in him is no sin. No one who lives in him keeps on sinning. ... Anyone who does not do what is right is not God's child, nor is anyone who does not love their brother and sister. For his is the message you heard from the beginning: We should love one another. Do not be like Cain, who belonged to the evil one and murdered his brother. ... We know that we have passed from death to life, because we love each other. Anyone who does not love remains in death. 1 John 3:1a, 4–6a, 10b–12a, 14

Be on your guard; stand firm in the faith; be courageous; be strong. Do everything in love. 1 Corinthians 16:13–14

The only thing that counts is faith expressing itself through love. Galatians 5:6b

The Bible makes it clear that we can be gifted and accomplished, that we can demonstrate faith and sacrifice, but if love is not our guiding motivation than nothing we do will be of lasting value (1

Corinthians 13:1–3). Learning to love, as God desires and teaches us to, is the most important aspect of our life. Meditate and talk to God about what you are learning about love. As we think about what God's idea of true love is, we start to realize how much we fall short without his help. The Holy Spirit of truth changing and directing us enables us to choose to love others step by step, and with God's help it becomes a way of life. Read through these verses again and write down anything God teaches you or that touches your heart. Write down any area or relationship he is prompting you to work on and ask him for his help. Commit to seek and listen to the Spirit of truth, who desires to teach us all about true love. Our lives will start to sparkle and God promises that though life may not be easy we will live happily ever after (1 Peter 1:3–6)!

Learning to Love Overcomes Sorrow

I found love with a freckled faced boy with a shy, yet mischievous smile. We found happiness in our time together, respected each other, and in the mountains over Monterey made a commitment to marry. Soon we had children and a house where I could see the rolling hills. It was a dream come true! OK, I admit, married life takes some adjustment, but this was it, a love that was true and that made me feel secure in this crazy world. Then that tragic day came, a terrible accident. Steve was not coming home to me. Daddy was not going to be able to come home and play with his little boy and baby girl as he had promised going out the door that morning. We were not going to go on vacation to Lake Tahoe next week. I saw his lifeless, blood-stained body and yet that evening I sat on the back steps overlooking his garden waiting for him, but he did not come. The man I relied on was no longer there to care for us. In an instant my whole life changed. I believed God cared, but my children needed their father. I loved him and missed him! I wanted someone to hold me and I felt so alone. As the first year passed my little boy worried he was forgetting his dad. The children longed for a father and suggested we should buy one at the store. If I found someone else, maybe that would dull the pain.

God was gracious and I married again two years later. God had answered my prayer, but my plan was not his. After Steve was gone, I had moved back to New York with the children to be near family. Now we were moving again to Florida, because my new husband was taking a new job. I was disappointed to move so far from my family again and everything was happening so fast. We were not communicating as I had hoped. Before long I felt rejected in my new marriage and longed to be loved. It was hard! God was about to teach me a new depth of true love, a sacrificial love! One day, as I sank to the floor and cried out to God in my pain, the light flowed in from the window and great comfort washed over me. God assured me and whispered, "Just love him." *But, but, I need to be loved!* "I love you," God whispered, "and now I ask you to love him." In that moment I felt God's deep love, and I am so thankful I listened, so thankful I did not quit in my pain. Though it has not always been easy, we have both learned so much about acceptance and love. Now we have been married for thirty years and enjoy a beautiful growing family. I became stronger and God turned my sorrow into something beautiful.

We can ask why God would allow so much bad to happen in our lives and in our world. He longs for us to come to him in our pain as he grieves with us. He wants our questions and our honesty, and he gently shows us how to navigate this world where pain and death is still part of our reality. No one can comfort me like my Father God does. I believe that Jesus wept with me and will wipe away my tears when I finally come home to him. As I experienced the Spirit's comfort, I learned to trust God even more, knowing he is good and seeing him care for my children and me over and over again. In that trust, though it is hard to understand *why* tragedy strikes, we discover more of God's transforming, healing power and love. God helps us handle the sorrows of our lives and heals our pain. And he promises something more, "beauty from the ashes," gifts in our own lives and in the lives of others, for everyone who wants to be his child (Roman 8:28)!

> For the Lord is good and his love endures forever; his
> faithfulness continues through all generations.
> Psalm 100:5

Group Discussion:

1. Have you ever had a fairy-tale idea about love that led to disappointment?
2. Share about a time when you felt God's presence or God's love in a special way.
3. In learning about God's definition of love, what made an impression on you?
4. What can we learn about love from The Parable of the Good Samaritan?
5. Read 1 John 4:7–21 together. What stands out to you in this passage?
    a. Where does love come from?
    b. What is the evidence of our relationship with God?
    c. How is God's love made complete in us? What does this mean?
    d. Why does perfect love drive out fear?
6. Has there ever been a time in your life when God was teaching you how to truly love another?

CHAPTER 4

Passion with Purpose

I took a step of love today,
Though part of me said, "No"!
I struggled to take this first small step,
But God helped my love to show.

Looking to Jesus with each new step,
Soon within me a passion grew.
I learned to listen to a truthful voice,
Since then my life's renewed!

"The thief comes only to steal and kill and destroy;
I came that they may have life—life in all
its fullness." John 10:10 (GNB)

To enjoy the warmth of a new spring day, to dance freely, to be loved, and to reach a lifetime goal are all reflections of living with passion. An abundant life, a life in all its fullness, is one that demonstrates thankfulness, enthusiasm, faithfulness, meaning, celebration, and most of all love. The God who created this world, who knows the past, present, and future, has a place and role in mind for each of us. God's all-encompassing, compassionate plan weaves the lives of people together throughout history. Everyone is looking for significance and meaning. We are designed this way for a purpose, and we can discover our unique roles as we discover our gifts and passions. Finding our purpose starts with small steps of love. Day to day we become more aware of acting in kindness and obedience to God, even when we don't feel like it. God honors those decisions in our lives, developing our character through them. As we respond to God, our hearts soften and we become more thankful and aware of his love. Often our feelings will follow our obedience and from there God will cultivate a passion within us. Our God-given purpose in life will be discovered and fueled by our God-given passions that develop as we interact with God and each other. Our passions and purpose motivate us to go forward and give us the strength to persevere. Our lives reflect the goodness of God as we take part in his dynamic, interactive plan of love!

The predominant meaning of the word *passion* has evolved in a fascinating sequence. The origin of the English word *passion* denotes *the sufferings of Jesus Christ between the night of the Last Supper and his death.* Merriam-Webster's Dictionary still lists this as the first meaning in the full definition (def. 1a), and the second, *suffering,* (def. 2) is now noted as obsolete. The third meaning, *the state or capacity of being acted on by external agents or forces,* (def. 3) we will consider further. And finally Webster lists *Emotion,* (def. 4a), and *Love,* (def. 5a), both listing sub-meanings with positive and negative connotations. (merriam-webster.com) Urban Dictionary's top contemporary definition states beautifully: *Passion is when you put more energy into something than is required to do it. It is more than just enthusiasm or excitement, passion is ambition that is materialized into action to put as much heart, mind, body and soul into something as possible* (urbandictionary.com). The progression of the meaning of the word passion mirrors the progression of developing healthy and meaningful passion within our lives. As child-like idealism fades, we grasp for meaning in life. Our realization of *Jesus' passion for us, demonstrated on the cross,* gives us new hope and renders eternal *suffering "obsolete"* for all who follow him. As we allow the Spirit of truth into our lives we can win *the battle that will come from external forces* that want to steal our passions with counterfeit love. We find God-given purpose and fulfillment as we learn to *love, demonstrated by action that we can put our heart, mind, body, and soul into.*

We could summarize the meaning of passion as *intense emotion or purpose compelling us to action.* We will never see a more intense emotion of love leading to any greater action of love than Jesus going to the cross for his creation! The book of Hebrews gives us a clue to Jesus' motivation—"He endured the cross, ignoring the shame, for the sake of the joy that was laid out in front of him, and sat down at the right side of God's throne" (Hebrews 12:2 CEB). This is good news, a joyful message! Though Jesus suffered terribly, on the third day he rose again to life. Jesus took the punishment for humankind, whom he loves passionately, to secure future *joy.* He suffered to give *us life,* abundant life and eternal life!!! The deceiving evil one, who manipulates the truth, tries to trick us into thinking God wants us to suffer as he suffered, rather than the truth that he was willing to suffer in our place. No one wants to follow a God who applauds our suffering and nothing is further from the truth! God loves us and wants the best for us. He wants us to be happy and cries with us in our sorrow! There are times we suffer in this world because evil is present among us; he may allow it knowing it will build our character and prepare us for our future. There are times when evil and free will come together with terrifying results, but be assured God carries the sorrows of the innocent and will bring judgment on those who pursue evil. There are other times we choose to suffer for the sake of others. God is not happy to see us suffer, but he allows it, knowing ultimately our sacrifices will help others find life and bring us joy. He wants us to have life to the fullest, a meaningful life! God won the battle that raged between good and evil on the cross so he could be present with us in the battle between good and evil which vies for our passions. His passion is us!

The battle between good and evil is active in influencing the passions we develop and it is important that we are aware. The third meaning listed in Webster's—*being acted upon by external agents or forces*—is something we have all experienced. For example, if a husband or wife has a passionate relationship with their spouse it is a wonderful and good gift from God. However, if they developed a passion for someone outside their marriage there may be an *external agent*, in this case an evil influence, at work trying to destroy their lives. A passion for our job is very positive, yet if that passion derails us from our family or God's plan it has a negative impact. We can develop a passion that is healthy or a passion that is harmful. We can pursue a passion motivated by greed or motivated by caring for others. Our own desires combined with temptations from outside influences or *forces* can affect what passions we develop. Is it lust or pure love? Is it arrogance or compassion? Discovering our passion and purpose, whether for good or bad, usually starts with small steps, so it is important to evaluate, *"Is it from the Spirit of truth or is it from the evil one?"*

When we begin to feel passion arise within us we should ask ourselves, *"What is its source?"* Our thoughts generate our feelings which influence our passions, not the other way around, as most people think. Since our feelings usually develop from our thoughts we need to guard them! As thoughts and ideas cross our minds we need to consider if they are ours alone, from the evil one, or from God. Discard quickly thoughts that are impure, violent, unkind, or that take offense. These types of thoughts are *never* from God. They steal from our lives and if given opportunity to take root they can ultimately destroy us. To have the power to guard our minds it is important to have a relationship with our living God, talking to him each day, reading and reflecting on his word, and aligning ourselves with his principles. We can send away and replace harmful thoughts by memorizing some of our favorite Bible verses or thinking about something good. "Finally, brothers and sisters, whatever is true, whatever is noble, whatever is right, whatever is pure, whatever is lovely, whatever is admirable—if anything is excellent or praiseworthy—think about such things" (Philippians 4:8). When we rely on the Spirit of truth to keep our thoughts positive, he will begin to stir a healthy passion within us that will connect us to others, as we follow his direction. This is the key to living a meaningful life— not a life without struggle, but rather a life really worth living and full of purpose. The Holy Spirit of truth wants to fuel our passions, motivating us to action that touches the lives of others. Our active response allows us to grow in maturity and discover God's will for our lives, ultimately bringing us joy!

When it comes to the opposing influences vying for our passions, the battle between good and evil is right at our doorstep. There are many things that can dull our senses or pull us away from what God has planned for our lives. One example is spending time with the wrong friends—people who continually influence us to think negatively or to make bad choices. Choose friends that encourage you to grow and care for others. Set limits on the time you spend with people who are discouraging or lead you to do what you know is wrong. God may use us in their lives, but we need to be at a place where we are strong in our commitment to love and follow God's best. Some other seductive examples prevalent in our society are video games, television, and time on the internet. If we are not careful to set boundaries, these will rob us of our time with others, lull us into living a life of apathy, and in some cases even teach immorality. Evil is tricky! That's why staying close to God is so important, so that we can discover what God's best is for our lives. Consider the activities in your life and ask God what is of value and what is wasting your precious time! The battle between good and evil is active in influencing who and what we pursue. Choose wisely and with an open heart toward God.

Our passions often develop in areas that will use our natural and spiritual gifts, which makes sense since God has given us both. Natural gifts are talents we are born with, yet still need our time and work to develop. We have a choice whether or not we cultivate them and whether we use them for good. Some examples are a beautiful voice, a mechanical ability, a gifted way with children, or a mind for business. Spiritual gifts are given by God to bring people to him and encourage each other. These gifts are developed as we use them in faith and some examples are wisdom, teaching, and healing (1

Corinthians 12). A positive change in our character, transforming us into a person of depth and beauty that will attract others, is also part of our spiritual gifting. "But the fruit of the Spirit is love, joy, peace, forbearance, kindness, goodness, faithfulness, gentleness and self-control" (Galatians 5:22–23a). Often our natural and spiritual gifts work together to accomplish our God-given purpose, and our passion fuels our efforts as we take steps forward to develop them. The gifts we are given in life, whether natural, spiritual, or material, grow as we use them to enhance the lives of others. This is one of God's basic principles. The Parable of the Talents teaches that God entrusts more to those who are faithful to use their gifts and abilities (Matthew 25:14–30). "Now it is required that those who have been given a trust must prove faithful" (1 Corinthians 4:2). God's plan is interactive. He has placed each of us in a time and place in history with the talents, gifts, and passion needed to accomplish his will. We have the choice whether or not we participate.

No one is an island when it comes to putting gifts and passions into action. Working together makes a world of difference as each person's gifts are used in unity to accomplish what God has planned. 1 Corinthians 12 and Romans 12 teach us that God gives us gifts to be used together for the common good. He created each of us for a specific purpose and gives us opportunity and free will to take part in his compassionate plan. Within a church (a group of people who follow Jesus) God often calls people with different gifts who are excited about similar ideas so that they can join God in what he plans to do. In unity they can accomplish what no one could do on their own. Look for others who are excited about doing something similar to what God has impressed upon your heart. By getting involved and working together you can learn and accomplish more than you ever could on your own. The passion God has developed within you may give you the voice to recruit others. Individuals and churches working together within a community delight God! Each church in a city may have a different role that God designed for them. Together, several churches can meet a wide array of needs within a community, bringing love and hope to the people who need it.

Another powerful way our gifts can be used together is when a whole family unites in a single passion to reach out and help others. Some of the most successful endeavors have started this way. However, if your spouse or family does not share your excitement about an idea that you feel God has placed on your heart, be careful to go slowly. Pray and ask God to give them the passion or to help you find another avenue to pursue yours. Be patience and wait on God. This may be a time of preparation for you. Look for people with similar dreams and partner with them, seeking your family's approval. As long as you are not neglecting your responsibility and are there when your family needs you, seeing your involvement can inspire them to seek God's purpose for their own lives. Supporting each other in our passions and dreams is glue for our relationships. When a family shares a dream and works together it is ideal, because we are spending time and growing together, causing us to love each other all the more. That love overflows!

Celebrate Together

Celebrations are also an important part of living life with passion. Planning something special to express our thankfulness and to cultivate our relationships adds joy to our lives. Time around a dinner table with love and laughter is so good for our souls! To live fully we need to take the time to appreciate each other and celebrate important milestones and events. In the Bible, God often instructed his people to set aside special times to celebrate and remember what he had done for them. Holidays and birthdays are important times of the year to get-together, demonstrate our love for each other, and express our thankfulness. Make the most of opportunities to bring joy into each other's lives. Appreciate the people who plan and work to make time together special. At times be mindful to include people you know who do not have family nearby. Our God enjoys our thankful celebration and delights in seeing us live joyfully!

Jesus' passion was to save us from evil! He won the battle on a cross and rose again from death to life after three days. "God has raised this Jesus to life, and we are all witnesses of it" (Acts 2:32). Jesus' resurrection is historical fact! He has ultimately defeated the power of sin and death. <u>The final outcome of the battle between good and evil is already decided!</u> <u>What's *not* decided is the effect your life will have on the battle! Decisions of action and inaction that you make each day, and the forces that influence your choices and fuel your passions will have an effect on our world.</u> Our choices affect the people with whom we come into contact. The first steps may be hard, but if you take them God will show you where you fit in his wonderful plan and your passions will develop. God offers eternal security by trusting Jesus and the sacrifice he made. It is a free gift! In turn he calls us to take part in bringing comfort and hope to the hurting people around us. Will you show love in practical and meaningful ways to the people you know? Will you gently warn those who give no regard to eternity that they are on a dangerous course? Will you help them turn and enjoy a relationship with God and eternal life? We have a reason to celebrate. We can have a passionate life, life in all its fullness, a life of love and purpose!

> "For I know the plans I have for you," declares the Lord, "plans to prosper you and not to harm you, plans to give you a hope and a future. Then you will call on me and come and pray to me, and I will listen to you. You will seek me and find me when you seek me with all of your heart." Jeremiah 29:11–13

> Many are the plans in a person's heart, but it is the Lord's purpose that prevails. Proverbs 19:21

> But the plans of the Lord stand firm forever, the purposes of his heart through all generations. Psalm 33:11

> As the rain and the snow come down from heaven, and do not return to it without watering the earth and making it bud and flourish... so is my word that goes out from my mouth: it will not return to me empty, but will accomplish what I desire and achieve the purpose for which I sent it. You will go out in joy and be led forth in peace; the mountains and the hills will burst into song and the trees of the field will clap their hands. Isaiah 55:10–12

A Passion is Born

I have a passion for people from every corner of the globe to know that Jesus loves them and is offering hope for a fulfilled and eternal life. As I look back, I can see how God has placed me in places and situations that have deepened my passion. For example, at one point in my life, a move we made landed us in an amazingly "missions-minded" church. This changed the way I thought about our world and also led to having two young women, one Turkish and one Egyptian, live with our family. Traveling to Europe, South America, and Asia with my family on vacation and with my husband's work helped me truly appreciate and enjoy other cultures. Most recently my volunteer work with international students further opened my heart and strengthened my passion for the world.

An amazing day in the summer of 2012 fueled my passion for the country of Turkey. During the spring I had traveled to Kazakhstan to visit some students with whom I had become friends while they were working summer jobs in the USA. While there, I met a young woman named Libby who had been healed of 4th stage Hodgkin's lymphoma and had lived for a year with a family in Turkey during her treatment. I got to know Libby when she came to the USA a few months later on her vacation as a volunteer in Ocean City. Just after Libby left, a young Turkish woman, Anna, who had lived a year with our family and was now a flight attendant, offered me a free trip with her to Istanbul. Anna had always wanted me to visit her country. Within a week I was on the plane excited about the opportunity to spend time with her and see Turkey! Sadly, Anna was called to cover another flight and had to leave me on my own in Istanbul, without any Turkish contacts. How I wished I knew the name of the family that Libby had stayed with, who spoke English! However, I was content to have God as my companion as I explored Istanbul and sat by the pool reading *The Circle Maker*, by Mark Batterson. As I read, I had the feeling God was asking me to circle the country of Turkey in prayer. *Well of course you are having that thought; you are reading the book The Circle Maker! God, are you really asking me to return to Turkey or is this one of my own crazy ideas? Please help me to know if you really want me to do it!* I went through the rest of the week without confirmation of the thoughts God had given me.

On my last full day in Istanbul, I was determined to find a church to visit. Earlier that week I discovered Union Church while searching on-line, located just off Istiklal in Taskim. It was on a long touristic street on the other side of the city, but I did not have the address. Sunday morning I was drawn to look for Union Church. I took the hotel shuttle bus to Taskim and right away was excited to see a building with a cross atop it. I thought it was the church and entered, not realizing it was the French consulate. The disgruntled guard stopped me, sending me on my way. I started down Istiklal Street, asking several people, but no one knew where the church was. With each passing block I became more discouraged, not knowing, literally or figuratively, where I was or where I was going. I began to pray silently, telling God how discouraged I felt, how I needed some kind of confirmation. *How could I return to travel around all of Turkey when I could not even find this church?!!* I asked God to help me and told him how I needed him to direct my life. Just then, I heard English voices and saw a couple walking beside me, so I asked if they knew where the church was. To my surprise they told me they had gone to an earlier service at Union Church and had walked up Istiklal to get money from the bank; they would be happy to show me the way! As we introduced ourselves, I told them I was from Ocean City in the USA. They said, "We know a young woman who traveled to Ocean City as a volunteer this summer." "Libby!" I exclaimed. They looked at me in amazement ... they were the couple who had taken care of her!!!

I had a strong sense of God's presence with me at church. The message was about how great, how deep and how amazing God's love is for each of us and for all people. After church I met a young woman and shared what had just happened. I also told her the name of a man I was hoping to meet while in Istanbul, but though I had tried to contact him I had not heard from him. She looked at me wide eyed; he was coming in just a few minutes to pick her up! Though it had been a sunny day it began to rain and hail just as he arrived so we had some time to talk in the covered courtyard. As the weather cleared and the sun returned, we left, and I made my way back to the bus just in time. I wanted to take a picture at a particular spot I had noticed earlier that showed the vast amount of people who live in Istanbul. At that spot the driver stopped. He motioned for me to get out, indicating in broken English that he would wait. How did he know I wanted a picture just at that spot when there was no special landmark there? I returned to the shelter of my hotel and as I entered the storm came up again with wind, rain, and hail. What a remarkable morning! I knew it had been orchestrated by God and it gave me confidence that he was directing me! I wrote down everything that had happened and then decided the day was not over.

The sun was shining again. I still had time to look for Saint Stephen's Church, which I wanted to do in honor of my late husband, Stephen. I heard it was not too far and got a taxi. The driver weaved in and out of narrow streets and stopped at a tall double door, like a solid gate, that was cracked open. I peeked inside and saw a man standing at a window in the courtyard. He had a basket of candles and offered me one and then directed me to the small chapel. I went forward to pray, alone in the stain glassed church. When I finished I arose to see a woman standing at the back, perfectly centered in the isle, with the light streaming in behind her. She had dark bobbed hair, wore a flared skirt, and she was holding a basket of grapes. She asked me if I would like to light my candle and showed me how. She spoke English and explained to me that this was not the only Saint Stephen's Church in the town. There were three! Actually, the town itself had been named Saint Stephen at one time. She pointed out the location of each church, but then left to meet her mother for tea. She had told me I could walk along the sea to get back to my hotel. I explored each church and then started back, enjoying the colorful fishing boats, the crisp air, and the pastel colored clouds billowing over the sea. The deep blue sky as a backdrop made the colors very vibrant after the storm. As I walked, full of joy, I heard the woman whom I had met at Saint Stephen's call out to me, "Hellooo." She had spotted me and asked if I would join them for tea. It was lovely! Three months later I returned to circle Turkey in prayer, a trip I will never forget. God gave me the gift of an amazing day and was fueling my passion for Turkey!

Group Discussion:

1. Have you ever taken a small step to obey God that helped you to learn something about yourself or your relationship with God? Tell us about it.
2. It is common to hesitate or talk ourselves out of taking a step of love. Why do you think this is true?
3. Why is it important to consider the source of passions that develop within us?
4. Is there activities or influences that are robbing you from a life of purpose and contentment? What steps could you take to pursue your relationship with God and to live a life of purpose?
5. Is there anything you are passionate about—an idea, cause, or concern for someone?
6. What is the difference between our natural gifts and our spiritual gifts? Do you believe both come from God? What do you think your talents or gifts are?
7. Perhaps by now you have had a chance to look at the alphabetic list of outreach ideas in the back of the book. Is there any idea that you are excited about and could see yourself doing?
8. Have you ever experienced a time you felt God was leading you to do something? What happened?

CHAPTER 5

Fighting Evil

Wonderful our world was created,
We were happy and loved at the start.
But evil seduced our free will,
Beginning the battle for hearts.

Now we're searching for purpose and meaning,
And we try to make sense of the fight.
More than a test, it's our pathway,
To find what is true and is right.

Malice and Magnificence opposing,
Battling for minds and for souls.
Humbly we realize we're helpless,
Until God's goodness is given control.

Finally be strong in the Lord and in his mighty power.
Put on the full armor of God so that you can take
your stand against the devil's schemes. For our

struggle is not against flesh and blood, but against the rulers, against the authorities, against the powers of this dark world and against the spiritual forces of evil in the heavenly realms. Ephesians 6:10–12

Action hero adventures, the classic Disney movies, and our favorite fairy tales all have one thing in common— the battle between good and evil. Often these stories suggest a spiritual aspect to the battle, something happening beyond that which we can see. They depict an evil entity with a dominating influence over the villains, actively seeking to deceive the good or innocence of the hero or heroine. Is there a cosmic battle raging between darkness and light? If we take an honest look at the world, our nightly world news, or our local headlines, it's there, a fight between good and evil that seems to defy logic. Think back in your own life. Have you ever made a bad decision based on deception? Don't get me wrong. We can make plenty on our own, for our own selfish reasons, but sometimes outside influences come into play. We believe a lie, which plays on our vulnerability or weakness, and we are pulled in a direction we thought we would never go. Then we begin to justify our attitudes and actions, not wanting to face our part, our guilt, and before long our hearts get a little harder. Now evil has the upper hand and we begin to believe wrong is right.

Don't underestimate what our lives contribute, one way or the other, to the battle and outcome of the ongoing war between good and evil. We are called to make an impact on evil within our homes, communities, and sometimes even our world. Just like in our favorite stories, love shows up in the midst of the battle and usually wins (always wins in the light of eternity), but often not without the battle intensifying first. We can have a part in this real life melodrama between good and evil when we set out to love others, making their needs as important as our own. When we decide to get off the side lines and take an active role, it gets the attention of the supernatural realm and evil may put up a stronger fight. As we actively reach out to others there will be opposition, but we should not fear it or let it derail us. We are not alone in the battle to show love to our world! We need help and we have it in God, his people, and even his angels. We can say as Elijah, "Don't be afraid. ... Those who are with us are more than those who are with them" (2 Kings 6:16). Jesus showed us over and over again he has been given authority over evil and he teaches us to call on his authority. Understanding this will help us continue in confidence because we are assured God has won the battle in the long run. If we are living to reflect God's love we are on the winning side!

When we set out to make a difference in our world, to show God's love and protection to others, we cannot fully prepare before going forward, and we cannot continue forward without further preparation. In other words, we must take a step of faith to join God in his work. We learn and are enabled step by step as we interact with God. That preparation and process is described in the book of Ephesians by the analogy of putting on armor, a picture taken from warfare: "Therefore put on the full armor of God, so that when the day of evil comes, you may be able to stand your ground, and after you have done everything, to stand. Stand firm then, with the <u>belt of truth</u> buckled around your waist, with the <u>breastplate of righteousness</u> in place, and with your <u>feet fitted with the readiness that comes from the gospel of peace</u>. In addition to all this, take up the shield of faith, with which you can extinguish all the flaming arrows of the evil one. Take the helmet of salvation and the sword of the Spirit, which is the word of God. And pray in the Spirit on all occasions with all kinds of prayers and requests. With this in mind be alert and always keep on praying for all the Lord's people" (Ephesians 6:13–18, emphasis mine). Let's look at each metaphor; practical instruction and protection that has proven effective in fighting evil. They also teach us much about our part in taking hold of God's provision in his unfolding plan for our world.

The Belt of Truth

In chapter two we explored the importance of the Spirit of truth. It should scare us how easily we can be led astray from reality or truth. Ideas are taught, even within religion, which can seem plausible but are not true and are not part of God's plan. Humankind is susceptible and our hearts can deceive us. That is why we need the Holy Spirit of truth to help us discern reality. That is why we must filter everything through the main precepts in the Bible—to love and rely on God and to love and care for each other. "Show me your ways, O Lord, teach me your paths; guide me in your truth and teach me, for you are God my Savior, and my hope is in you all day long" (Psalm 25:4–5). Jesus said that the reason he was born and came in to this world was to testify to truth (John 18:37). Over and over again he says, throughout the book of John, "I tell you the truth," and then challenges our thinking in order to set us free. God created this complex world and he is the ultimate source of truth. We can start to be fortified by truth as we deal with negative and unloving areas in our own lives. Talk to God about your struggles and ask him to show you truth. Let him know when you are sorry and need his help to make a change. Accept the grace and forgiveness Jesus offers us. <u>If you have never accepted the sacrifice Jesus made by going to the cross to pay for your sin, go ahead and claim it for yourself.</u> <u>It is at this point that you will have the Spirit of truth available to you!</u>

The Breastplate of Righteousness

Righteousness protects our hearts as a breastplate of armor would. When we receive the forgiveness Jesus offers us, acknowledging his payment for our sin, God then sees us as righteous. God says that he no longer remembers our sins or holds them against us (1 John 1:9, Hebrews 8:12). This is the true protection from death and evil—<u>Jesus' righteousness applied to us!</u> Just as a shield protects our heart from a fatal wound, Jesus' righteousness protects us from evil and spiritual death. <u>This is the first and most important aspect of the "breastplate of righteousness" because without it we do not have access to the second, which is becoming righteous.</u> The Comforter and Counselor, namely the Holy Spirit of truth, whom Jesus told us would come can now partner with us in life. The Holy Spirit will teach us to be strong, yet gentle; to have innocence, and yet be wise. He will help us to find the truth so we better understand what Jesus would do in the situations of our lives.

The Bible gives us a picture lesson to help us learn about righteousness. In the book of Exodus (Exodus 20 and 32–34), after Moses delivered his people from slavery he received the Ten Commandments on Mount Sinai to guide his people. God himself met with Moses for forty days in a cloud upon the mountain, giving him instructions for his people to live righteously. As Moses made his way down the mountain, he could see that the people had already turned from the God who had just delivered them from slavery! They were worshiping a golden calf—already breaking the first commandment that God had just given Moses. In his anger Moses threw the tablets, breaking them. The broken tablets are a picture lesson that the law would be broken and thus bring death before Holy God. About three thousand people were killed in the judgment that followed. God called Moses, who was fervently praying for God's mercy, to go back up the mountain. Moses was on Mt. Sinai for another forty days and nights, and once again God gave to him the Ten Commandments. The two new tablets of the Law, inscribed by God, were then carried down and stored in the Ark of the Covenant. God was determined to show compassion and love and made a covenant with the people. If they would trust and obey by following his law to love God and each other, he would bless them (Deuteronomy 10, 11). However, even when they knew what God expected, they still failed in their efforts to meet their part of the covenant promise. Before Moses died at one hundred and twenty years old, God renewed his covenant with the people, including new generations (Deuteronomy 28–30). The Old Testament goes on to record that God sent many prophets to his people and they tried over and over again to follow God's law, but always failed! In the same way, as we strive to follow God's law—to love each other and do the right thing—in our own strength we fail. Our failure helps us to understand that we need help. God has a plan to keep both sides of the covenant promise.

The picture story continues in the New Testament book of Acts, but first let's set the stage as God takes action to keep our part of the covenant. Jesus, born of the Virgin Mary, lived on earth until age thirty-three, teaching men the true meaning of God's law and performing many miracles of compassion, including raising people from the dead. To fulfill his destiny, he was falsely accused and willingly put to death by crucifixion to pay for *our* sins. Jesus' purpose was to make it possible for men and women to be declared righteous before God and receive the help of the Holy Spirit of truth. (At that point in time, humankind did not comprehend God's redemptive plan that was unfolding.) Death could not hold Jesus in the tomb; after all he is the Creator (John 1:3). On the third day, though the tomb was sealed and guarded, the giant stone rolled from the entrance. Jesus was and he is alive! Scripture tells us he met with and comforted his followers and over five-hundred people were eyewitnesses to his resurrection (1 Corinthians 15:3–6). Jesus told them about the kingdom of God and to expect the Spirit of truth (which they also did not yet understand). Forty days after the resurrection his followers watched as Jesus ascended to heaven. Just before rising into the clouds he gave them the great commission and his assurance: "All authority on heaven and on earth has been given to me. Therefore go and make disciples of all nations, baptizing them in the name of the Father, and of the Son, and of the Holy Spirit, teaching them to obey everything I have commanded you. And surely I am with you always, to the very end of the age" (Matthew 28:19–20).

Our picture story continues in Acts 2. On the holy day of Pentecost, which was celebrated to commemorate Moses receiving the Ten Commandments, the promised Holy Spirit of truth arrived. People from every nation were gathered in Jerusalem. The crowd heard a great wind and saw fire landing upon each person, and yet not harming them! Jesus' followers began to speak languages they did not know and the people gathered could hear what was being said in their own language. Peter spoke, quoting from the prophet Joel; "In the last days, God says, I will pour out my Spirit on all people ..." (Acts 2:17). About three thousand people realized that Jesus was the promised Savior and received eternal life! Three thousand souls received life, the same number of people who died when the Law was given (Exodus 32:28, Acts 2:41)! From this day forward in history, the Spirit of truth, God himself, is available to dwell with us, teaching us to love and giving us first-hand help in the battle against sin and evil. <u>The law itself could not make us righteous, but God, dwelling within human hearts, can!</u> The law could not cause our hearts to love unselfishly, but the Spirit of God can.

> So now there isn't any condemnation for those who are in Christ Jesus. The law of the Spirit of life in Christ Jesus has set you free from the law of sin and death. God has done what was impossible for the Law, since it was weak because of selfishness. God condemned sin in the body by sending his own Son to deal with sin in the same body as humans, who are controlled by sin. He did this so that the righteous requirements of the Law might be fulfilled in us. Now the way we live is based on the Spirit, not based on selfishness. Romans 8:1-4 (CEB)

> You show that you are Christ's letter... You weren't written with ink but with the Spirit of the living God. You weren't written on tablets of stone but on tablets of human hearts. This is the confidence we have through Christ in the presence

of God. It is not that we ourselves are qualified to claim that anything came from us. No, qualification came from God. He qualifies us as ministers of a new covenant, not based on what was written but on the Spirit, because what is written kills, but the Spirit gives life. 2 Corinthians 3:3-6 (CEB)

Thus our righteousness is twofold, because now we can be proclaimed righteous by God and we also have help to become righteous through the Holy Spirit's presence in our lives. We have the help we need to do the right thing, to make good choices, and to obtain the comfort our hearts so need, if we choose to embrace it. The Spirit helps us not to judge as we apply the grace and love of God to others that we ourselves have received. Once God reveals truth to us, there will be adjustments to make on our part. To go forward in confidence we will need to change, aligning ourselves to what God teaches us through his word. Our righteousness is found only in Christ, who frees us from sin and guilt. Freedom is found *not* in following a list of rules and regulations, but rather in aligning our hearts with the heart of God by the Spirit of truth. God is love; he is pure and just and reaches out to imperfect humans with longsuffering and grace. He desires for us to accept his grace and love, and extend it to others, becoming heroes in the battle between good and evil.

Feet Fitted with the Readiness that Comes from the Gospel of Peace

God tells us that our life on earth can be like running a race for him (Hebrews 12:1, 1 Corinthians 9). To run the race we need to be fitted with the right shoes—the gospel of peace. Jesus' sacrificial

<u>death and victorious resurrection on our behalf enables sinful men</u> <u>and women to find peace with God.</u> <u>This is the gospel of peace!</u> We need to "put on" this gospel, wearing it so that others might also see the truth and light living in us as we run the race we have been given. Jesus explained to us that he did not come so we would have peace on earth at the present time, as many of his followers thought, but rather that we could have peace with God through his death and resurrection. <u>We need to be at peace with our Creator in order to</u> <u>have peace with others.</u> Trusting him and putting on the gospel of peace prepares us to run the race with our feet equipped. We are no longer fighting or hiding from God in our rebellious state, but can choose to work or run alongside him. We are on his team and he longs to help us in our race, giving us strength and endurance along the way. Just as in a relay, we run our part of the race, passing on and proclaiming the good news of Jesus' redemption and peace to the people along our path of life, who in turn go forward, passing true love to future generations.

The Shield of Faith

Do you believe in God? Do you believe he created the universe? Do you believe in his promises? Do you want to believe? Our faith in God (and what he teaches us in his word and by experience), is what brings us to the point of believing the gospel of peace, the good news of Jesus. Faith means we believe or at least that we desire to believe God is there for us. We desire a relationship with God enough to seek him! Though we cannot see God, we believe that he exists from the evidence of creation, the love of his people, and through our experiences as we learn to trust him. "And without faith it is impossible to please God, because anyone who comes to him must believe that he exists and that he rewards those who earnestly seek him" (Hebrews 11:6). <u>Faith is believing God wants the best for us and can be trusted completely.</u> <u>It is acknowledging his power and trusting his love.</u> We believe he loves us and was willing to come from heaven to lay down his life in order to rescue us. This faith is our shield from death and from all that the evil one sends our way. Faith calls on the power and protection of God and grows as we experience his provision. God allows difficulties in our lives because we learn to trust, to love, and to grow in wisdom from them. Faith helps us to persevere in life through the hard times. Our faith increases as we experience God's help and care for us. His love gives us the spiritual hope and strength we need to go forward. God also gives an extra measure of faith as a gift to help others as we pray and act on their behalf. Faith, demonstrated by our prayers for others, provides a shield from the attacks of evil. When we live in active faith, we find protection and courage to fight the good fight, living for God and caring for those around us!

The Helmet of Salvation

A helmet protects you from a blow to the head, a fatal blow. <u>Faith in the gospel of peace brings you salvation, saving you from spiritual death, which is an eternal separation from God.</u> God is the source of true love and light, so that separation would mean no love and no light, only darkness and sorrow. The Bible teaches that the blood of Jesus—the Son of God and the Son of Man, the perfect and sinless lamb—is applied to our lives when we turn to him for salvation. It covers us, just as the blood of a lamb without defect was applied to the door frame of the Hebrew people at Passover, so that death passes over (Exodus 12). But Jesus' blood was poured out for all people, from every race and nation under heaven. <u>The Bible makes it clear that God wants all people to turn to him and be saved from eternal death.</u> "The Lord is not slow in keeping his promise, ... Instead he is patient with you, not wanting anyone to perish, but everyone to come to repentance" (2 Peter 3:9). God the Father is waiting for you to believe that Jesus died for you! The Holy Spirit is calling out to you to accept the free gift of salvation. Don't allow evil to strike a fatal blow to your life; put on the helmet of salvation. Without it we do not have protection from death or the power necessary to successfully fight evil in our own lives and on behalf of the lives of others.

The Sword of the Spirit, which is the Word of God

<u>God speaks to us through his word, the Bible.</u> <u>The word of God is often the source the Spirit of truth uses to change us for the better and improve our relationships.</u> The Holy Spirit prompts us to act as we learn who God is and what he wants both for us and from us. The Spirit shows us areas where we do not trust God and where we are not showing compassion and love to others. <u>If we spend time thinking about what God is saying to us, and then adjust our lives to it, God will prepare us to live well and help others find life.</u> The Bible can be overwhelming at first, yet from beginning to end it is the story of God's enduring love for the people he created. It tells of God's unfailing, sacrificial love and his plan to redeem humankind! The Bible gives us practical instructions for our relationships and our quest to live fulfilled. It is a book with many layers and stories within

the story that only God could weave, though it was written by forty different authors from many walks of life. Each writer, reflecting his individual personality, was inspired by God and assisted by the Holy Spirit to write truth. In this way God gave his message to the world. Over and over again, people who earnestly study the Bible increase in their faith in God because it would be impossible for this book to be so amazingly cohesive without God's supernatural direction. The living word of God has amazing power to change lives. Read it chapter by chapter, even verse by verse. Ask God to teach you and marvel at the way he reveals the truth to you in the days ahead! Memorize your favorite verses; it is amazing how they will pop into your mind just when you need them! God's word, like a sword, will fight off evil that is seeking to influence your mind, your heart, and ultimately your life. Try starting with the book of John if you are new to reading the Bible. Ask God to help you discover *his* plan for your life. "All scripture is God-breathed and is useful for teaching, rebuking, correcting and training in righteousness, so that the servant of God may be thoroughly equipped for every good work" (2 Timothy 3:16). "For the word of God is alive and active. Sharper than any double edged sword, it penetrates even to dividing soul and spirit, joints and marrow; it judges the thoughts and attitudes of the heart" (Hebrews 4:12). <u>We need instruction from the word of God to learn truth, live righteously, grow in faith, and to fight evil! The Spirit of truth helps us to understand and follow God's word.</u>

Prayer and Fighting Evil

The apostle Paul, in the book of Ephesians, explains the necessity of believers wearing spiritual armor and continues on with the following instruction: "And pray in the Spirit on all occasions with all kinds of prayers and requests. With this in mind be alert and always keep on praying for all the Lord's people" (Ephesians 6:18). The Lord's people are any followers of Jesus, doers of God's work. Prayer plays an important role in the life of God's people. There is evil raging a battle designed to keep people in darkness so we need to pray and ask others to pray for us. As God calls us, we need to call on God! When you see others doing God's good work pray for them! God's design is partnership with humanity. <u>Prayer welcomes the Holy Spirit's presence to the situation and helps to block the access of evil in the spiritual realm.</u> Praying is the first step to getting involved in the action, because if God is not with us we have already lost. Prayers for people who are far from God soften their hearts and help them to understand truth. Like God's word, it is both armor and weapon for fighting the good fight. Over the years I have heard many stories of people being moved to pray for someone at what seemed like an odd time, only later to find out that the person was in a difficult or dangerous situation just at that hour. Jesus is interceding for us, on our behalf, and the Spirit of God whispers, calling us to help and to pray! We must constantly call on and rely on God to be effective in our homes, communities, and our world.

"Let your gentleness be evident to all. The Lord is near. Do not be anxious about anything, but in every situation, by prayer and petition, with thanksgiving, present your requests to God. And the peace of God, which transcends all understanding, will guard your hearts and minds in Jesus Christ" (Philippians 4:5–7). Think about these verses. When we become anxious or frightened, or feel things are not in our control, that is when we are most likely to become angry, lash out, lose our patience, or do something we will regret. We need to remember the truth that God is near and wants to help us; believe it! Having this assurance will motivate us to talk to him about the situation and to rely on him, allowing the Holy Spirit to pour out gentleness through us.

Jesus taught us about prayer, primarily recorded in Luke 11:1–13, 18:1–14, Matthew 6:5–15 and Mark 9:28–29. He taught us that our appreciation, love, and respect for God and our commitment to his will is a good place to start. Asking for his help with our personal needs, asking for the needs of others, asking for forgiveness, forgiving others, and asking for protection from evil, is all a part of effective prayer. Jesus also taught us to be persistent and bold in prayer. John 17 records Jesus' prayer for his followers both for the present time and also those who would follow him in the future. Take some time to reflect on these verses and also look for other times when Jesus prays in the Bible. Jesus took time to get away to talk and listen to the Father. He prayed publicly and privately, for himself, for others, and for us. Jesus still prays for us (Romans 8:34)! Jesus prayed when he lived among us and still prays in heaven; not only did he teach about the importance of prayer, but he set an example.

Praying with the right motive and taking action when we are called to is very important. Jesus warns that prayer should never be uttered to impress others. In Isaiah 58, Matthew 6:5–17, and Luke 18:9–14 God warns that prayer without turning our heart to God and being obedient to care for the people he puts in our path is not effective. Prayer to make oneself *look* righteous is meaningless. However, the prayer of someone who earnestly seeks God and cares for others is very powerful. Though we will experience many answers to prayer, we may not always see the answer within our lifetime. God teaches us to be persistent and have confidence; we will have many wonderful surprises waiting to be discovered in eternity!

Commit to live for God. Prepare yourself for the battle between good and evil that is active at this present time in our world. Put on the armor of protection: truth, righteousness, the gospel of peace, faith, salvation, learning the word of God and applying it, and prayer. <u>We all have the opportunity to take hold of the protection that God provides for us from evil and apply it to our lives.</u> Ask and look to the Spirit of truth to direct you each day. Live your life ready to fight for good, reaching out to those around you in love. Living for God is living for love!

God's Word Protecting Hearts and Minds

Gracia Burman, in her book *In the Presence of My Enemies*, shared about her kidnapping in the Philippine jungles, along with her husband and others. Throughout a year, the Burmans moved from place to place with their captors, in the face of frequent gunfire and horrible conditions. Still, at times God helped them to reach out to their enemies. She tells how reciting the word of God and singing hymns is often what kept them going. This excerpt tells about a time they heard God's word on the short wave radio.

"On May 20, Martin got up the nerve to ask to borrow Sabaya's radio. Searching the dial for Voice of America to get the news, he happened upon KNLS, a Christian station out of Alaska. A short devotional came on, only two or three minutes. The pastor, named Andy Baker, read from Romans 8: 'If God is for us who can be against us? He who did not spare his own Son, but gave him up for us all—how will he not also, along with him, graciously give us all things? Who will bring any charge against those whom God has chosen? It is God who justifies. Who is he that condemns? Christ Jesus, who died—more than that, who was raised to life—is at the right hand of God also interceding for us.' (Romans 8:31–34) *'...if you are in the midst of a hard situation,' Pastor Baker said, 'and if you could hear Christ in the next room praying, you wouldn't be afraid of thousands of enemies. He would be calling your name.'* Martin and I looked at each other with tears in our eyes. The speaker than began to lead in prayer—for people who were oppressed, people on the West Bank and in Afghanistan, and people who were being treated wrongly because of their faith in Christ. It seemed like he was praying for us. We were overwhelmed." (pp. 255–256)

Group Discussion:

1. What are some examples of the battle between good and evil in our world?
2. Who does the Bible tell us is our true enemy? Why is this important to remember?
3. Describe each part of the armor God made available to us and how it helps in fighting evil.
    a. Belt of truth
    b. Breastplate of righteousness
    c. Feet fitted with the gospel of peace
    d. Shield of faith
    e. Helmet of salvation
    f. Sword of the Spirit which is the word of God
4. What part does prayer play in the fight between good and evil, in our lives and in our world?
5. Read Luke 11:1–13 and 18:1–14 together. What did Jesus teach us about prayer? (Perhaps each participant could name one thing.)
6. Read Isaiah 58:2–11. What are some possible reasons that God may not answer our prayers?
7. Describe a time when you felt caught up in the battle between good and evil.

CHAPTER 6

Our Words Matter

The melody of positive words,
Calming my stormy soul,
Saving me from waves of pain,
Helping me keep control.

Insecurity tries to drown me,
Pulling me from the light,
But loving words uphold me;
Their song is true and right.

"For the mouth speaks what the heart is full of. A good man brings good things out of the good stored up in him, and an evil man brings evil things out of the evil stored up in him. But I tell you that everyone will have to give an account on the day of judgment for every empty word they have spoken."
Matthew 12:34b–36

ur words have power! Proverbs 18:21 tells us they have the power of life and death. What we say to others can build them up or tear them down, show love or hate, express care or indifference. Our words *will* have an effect on others. Kind words fill our souls and encourage us to keep going. Evil words are full of lies and cause people to feel unloved. The power of words for good or bad, for proclaiming truth or planting insecurity and deception should not be underestimated. The Spirit of truth provides us help in both learning and practicing to speak in a truthful and loving way. Our words have the potential to comfort, guide, and empower others as we speak kind words of truth and share our experiences. God calls us to speak truth into the lives of people around us, people of all ages and every walk of life—words of truth chosen in love.

We started the discussion about the powerful effect that truth has on our life in chapter two. In our world truth can be hard to find. People can lie as easily as they tell the truth. Curiosity.discovery. com reports on the question: How often does the average person lie? "Some people lie all the time—for compulsive liars, telling a falsehood is a default action. But for a stab at a more reasonable number, we can look at a study conducted by University of Massachusetts researcher Robert Feldman, which demonstrates how reflexive the act of lying is for many people. In the study, which was published in the Journal of Basic and Applied Psychology, Feldman and his team of researchers asked two strangers to talk for 10 minutes. The conversations were recorded, and then each subject was asked to review the tape. Before looking at the footage, the subjects told researchers that they had been completely honest and accurate in their statements, but once the tape rolled, the subjects were amazed to discover all the little lies that came out in just 10 minutes. According to Feldman, 60 percent of the subjects lied at least once during the short conversation, and in that span of time, subjects told an average of 2.92 false things... In studies in which children have been observed in social interactions, 4-year-olds fibbed at least once every two hours, while six-year-olds could only make it 90 minutes before spinning a falsehood."

Pairs of strangers who engaged in conversation were amazed at how many times they were not accurate in their statements. "Most people lie in everyday conversation when they are trying to appear likable or competent," according to Feldman's study. It is more difficult than we admit, even to ourselves, to tell the truth, yet our truthful and encouraging words are just what our world needs. It is natural for us to focus on ourselves and therefore try to build ourselves up in the eyes of others, yet God wants us to be humble and focus on the interests of others (Philippians 2:3–8). We can see from this report that being completely truthful (and also transparent at times when it is beneficial to others) does not come naturally. We need the help of God to focus on the person we are with, rather than ourselves, and to speak truthfully with love.

The overriding principle when it comes to our words is to speak words that are truthful and build people up, rather than tear them down. "Do not let any unwholesome talk come out of your mouths, but only what is helpful for building others up according to their needs, that it may benefit those who listen" (Ephesians 4:29). Looking for the good in people and expressing encouragement and appreciation have a powerful effect. A recent study by Dr. Lisa Williams, a Lecturer in Psychology at the University of New South Wales, Australia claims, "Saying 'thank you' starts new friendships, reminds us of bonds, and maintains older relationships." Showing appreciation builds friendships and encourages perseverance. Expressing thankfulness proved to make a difference in establishing and maintaining relationships—evidence that our words matter.

Truthful, affirming words help to push away thoughts that are negative, untrue, and destructive. If you notice something good, a kindness, a talent, or a gift someone displays, tell them. You never know how much they may need your encouragement. Other times this means asking God to help us to say hard things in the most graceful and loving way, so that there is no mistake that we really care about the person we are speaking to. God may use us to guide someone away from deception or an unhealthy lifestyle. All of us at times need our thought life to be refocused on truth, rather than negativity or deception. There are many sources of lies in our world, pulling us down, increasing our insecurity, and at times drawing us into despair. We cannot make good decisions if we are basing our choices on lies. "… Jesus said, 'If you hold to my teachings … Then you will know the truth and the truth will set you free'" (John 8:31–32). Words have the power to help people find the truth and to let them know they are valued. Sharing our experiences about times when we have looked to God for help gives others hope that they can have the help they need to make good choices and fight temptation. Establishing trust can lead to relationships of accountability that help to keep us true. Our words are a very effective tool for bringing transformation, freedom, and love into the lives of others.

When we reach out with positive words of love, people will be attracted to us. The world longs for positive people who are both truthful and encouraging. People will come to us with problems, ask us for advice, and want our opinion. They have already decided we will do our best to tell them the truth. Don't let that overwhelm you, since God is with you to help. When someone approaches you, give them your respect and full attention. Making eye contact is important. Looking at something else, such as a cell phone or someone else across the room for instance, gives the wrong message. It is easy to be distracted; listening and staying focused takes practice as we take time to get to know people. Hear their concerns and fears, their hopes and dreams. Listening is the priority, being mindful to consider their words carefully. Try not to make assumptions about what someone is saying. Ask questions to clarify and understand. Pray, even if just a brief silent prayer, for God to help you to respond wisely. Even when we know God's word on a matter, God understands their situation far better than we do. We need God to help us communicate effectively to their situation and background. For example God may prompt us to ask the right question or to provide words of comfort. It is important to maintain confidentiality by *never* repeating private matters that someone felt comfortable enough to share, unless it is absolutely necessary as a matter of safety. The Holy Spirit wants to use us to speak truth into people's lives. He asks us to reflect his love. Will we be used by God or get in the way? "The words of the reckless pierce like swords, but the tongue of the wise brings healing" (Proverbs 12:18). What can we say or do to encourage this precious person before us? If appropriate, ask if they would like you to pray with them. Even if we are unable to pray *with* them, we can still pray for their needs, which may be one reason God has you involved in the first place; prayer makes a difference! On our own we cannot solve people's problems, but God is able and he longs to use our words to help bring wisdom and healing to others.

Words Trigger Our Emotions

There are many situations where words can calm things down and bring good or escalate the problem and bring sorrow. We need to rely on the Holy Spirit to know when to be silent and when to speak. "The one who has knowledge uses words with restraint, and whoever has understanding is even-tempered" (Proverbs 17:27). If we speak in anger or pride it will have negative, damaging results. If we speak encouraging words of love and forgiveness, it is life giving (Proverbs 10:11). "'In your anger do not sin': Do not let the sun go down while you are still angry, and do not give the devil a foothold. Do not let any unwholesome talk come out of your mouths, but only what is helpful for building others up according to their needs, that it may benefit those who listen" (Ephesians 4:26–27, 29). The people who are closest to us are also the people who can trigger the deepest emotions and therefore we need to be especially careful. When we disagree, speaking with gentleness and not allowing offense to take root protects us. God can help us speak calmly and to avoid lashing out. Take the time to understand each other's heart and needs, communicating with patience. How we speak to others is a reflection of our maturity, especially when it comes to those closest to us. Even if you feel being kind is one-sided, don't let that stop you from controlling your speech. Ask God for help. It is important to stop a negative cycle that can destroy a relationship. Our thoughts are affected by what we hear, so remember how much God values you, and step back to evaluate attacks. Often we are hurt by a misunderstanding. Is there truth, did I misunderstand, is this an area where we need to agree to disagree, or is this a tool of manipulation? If seeking the source of the problem or breaking a negative pattern seems impossible, don't be afraid to ask for help from a trusted counselor. Ultimately love never fails!

Our Reaction to Words Matters

"A person's wisdom yields patience; it is to one's glory to overlook an offense" (Proverbs 19:11). The first step to choosing words that will help a situation is *not* allowing ourselves to take offense. People will hurt us with their words, but our reaction can have an amazing effect. Saying something kind in return and showing humility builds relationships, but speaking with a defensive attitude tears them down. Inevitably we will hurt people too! Hearing words of forgiveness and encouragement when we have hurt someone heals us. Words of grace can help us find the courage to take responsibility for our attitude and actions. Words of forgiveness soothe our souls and help us know we are still valued and loved (2 Corinthians 2:7–8). If we allow ourselves to let an insult take harbor in our minds it is easier for evil to entrap us. Soon we become the accuser and hate can take root in our lives.

Words of Understanding

God tells us there is no need to be anxious in life and asks us to bring all our concerns to him (Philippians 4:6). Yet in our demanding and sometimes frightening world it is common to feel mounting pressure, fear, and a lack of control. When we face anxiety or feel overwhelmed, words of understanding comfort us and help us to keep going forward. "Anxiety weighs down a heart, but a kind word cheers it up" (Proverbs 12:25). Kind words can calm us down and help give us the confidence and security we need to take the next step. When we are grieving or facing disappointment, words of comfort let us know we are not alone. Someone empathizing with our situation or loss helps us to feel cared for. God longs to use us to give words of comfort to those who are mourning and broken. "Praise be to the God and Father of our Lord Jesus Christ, the Father of compassion and the God of all comfort, who comforts us in all our troubles, so that we can comfort those in any trouble with the comfort we ourselves have received from God" (2 Corinthians 1:3–4). Kind words remind us that God loves us; he is in control and wants to care for us. Be careful not to use platitudes that often leave an empty feeling, rather, acknowledge the difficulty of what someone is facing. Understanding words help to lift our spirits and give us a sense of peace.

Talking with Children

Children need to know they are loved and valued by God and also what God expects of them. Growing up is not easy; children face a wide array of challenges as they learn to comprehend and navigate the world around them. Naturally, they will have times when they are unsure of themselves and need our words of direction and encouragement. They need to know they can talk to God directly for guidance and help. As a parent or caregiver we need to guide and teach them by speaking the truth in love. Otherwise, how will they learn foundational truths? By watching TV and searching the internet? When they go to school or participate in sports they may not even hear there is a God who loves them, because many school systems today are directed not to mention God. The lessons of hard work, perseverance, and team building need to stand on a foundation of integrity. Our children may learn about character, but how frustrating if they never hear about the loving God who works within us to help us make good choices and have victory over our failures. All of history illustrates that those who try to live by the rules, without God's personal help, fail at a life of love and those who live lawlessly, live in chaos. We can encourage children to turn to God for the help and comfort we need in life, giving them an anchor in this unpredictable world. Jesus said that a child's simple faith is what we all need. How sad to think some children may never hear who to have faith in—the loving God, who is worthy of our trust!

Every child of God is valuable and unique. Telling a child they are important to God, and also to us, will bless them. We also need to teach children that all people are unique and gifted and help them to look for the gifts and talents of others. Encourage them to use their gifts together. If we model words of love and respect, as they grow up their relationships will be stronger. Our words can help them to look outside themselves and become aware of the gifts and needs of others. Children need to be taught that putting others first significantly adds to their own value.

There are some words commonly used by parents that may cause more harm than good—"I am your parent, not your friend." These words are tricky, because the opposite of friend in most people's minds is enemy. In the first six to ten years of life, most likely you *are* your child's closest friend as they learn to live in this overwhelming world, so do not allow evil to plant lies in your child's mind as they grow up. Choose your words carefully. "As for parents, don't provoke your children to anger, but raise them with discipline and instruction about the Lord" (Ephesians 6:4 CEB). Discipline and guide your children consistently, as we are all born with a selfish side in our nature and they will be lost without your correction. However, it's okay to be a friend to your child within the parental context of authority and protection; discipline is much more effective within a healthy, loving, and trusting relationship! After all, that is how God deals with us. He longs for us to trust him and to consider him our friend, yet he is our Father and knows what's best for us and does not hesitate to give us the discipline we need along the way.

The words we speak to our children can have a profound effect on their lives. Words of encouragement, instruction, and blessing, backed up by our example and loving care will help our children to be happy, healthy, and ready to face the world. "Fix these words of mine in your hearts and minds [to love and obey God] … Teach them to your children, talking about them when you sit at home and when you walk along the road, when you lie down and when you get up" (Deuteronomy 11:18–19).

Words that Build Dreams

When we have a dream, but it seems unobtainable, encouraging words can make the difference between success and failure. Everyone needs someone who believes in them, even if it is a stranger; without encouragement we may give up on our dreams. We may need a sounding board or someone to brainstorm with. We can be the person who helps someone take the next step of action on the path to fulfilling their goals and purpose in life. Don't allow your skeptical words to squelch the dreams of others, but encourage others to follow their hearts and work through the obstacles. Our friends and family are blessed when they know we are behind them. Our support, prayers, and encouragement may be just what someone needs to give them the hope and perseverance to succeed! "Now to him [God] who is able to do immeasurably more than we ask or imagine, according to his power that is at work within us,"... (Ephesians 3:20).

Follow Through

Our words must be backed up by our actions—follow through with what you say. Building trust is the foundation of a relationship; therefore we must be true to our word, saying only what we will *do* (within the boundaries of what is good and right). For example: if you say you will help someone move, then be sure to show up on moving day. If you say you believe in a principle, let your life reflect it. Everyone falls short, but to the very best of our ability, we should do what we say or don't say it. If circumstances change and you are unable to follow through, be sure to communicate the reason why. It is easy to say we will help or pray for someone and then forget to or never make the time. (When appropriate, praying for someone at the time you are with them is a good practice.) Jesus tells the parable of the two sons in Mathew 21:28–31. A father asked his sons to work in the vineyard. One son answered, "'I will not,'... but later he changed his mind and went." The other son answered politely "'I will, sir,' but he did not go." Jesus warns us it is the action that counts. True followers of Jesus know the importance of following through with what they say and also look to God to give them the strength and means to do it. Be reliable and ask God to help you live a life of integrity.

The evil one wants us to believe lies such as, *"You are worth nothing, more money will solve everything, or God is unreliable."* When we take the time to encourage and listen to each other—our friends, neighbors, spouse, children, or parents—we can be used of God to tell each other the truth. We can share how God has helped us when we were in a difficult situation or how we found healing after the inevitable grief that we all face at one time or another in this fallen world. "The tongue that brings healing is a tree of life, but a deceitful tongue crushes the spirit" (Proverbs 15:4 NIV © 1985). Learn to be intentional about what you say. You have the power to give life to others. Don't be afraid to use it; don't be afraid to speak words of truth and encouragement when God calls you to do so. We *can* help others to know they are valuable and loved by God through our loving and insightful words.

Encouraging Words that Made a Difference

In hopeful desperation a young woman who was in a difficult marriage went with her husband for counseling. She had been sincerely trying to keep her family together, but in her naivety always felt at fault (the evil one is a master at making us feel accused). At the time her husband was not willing to face how his drug abuse was affecting their family and his own mind. As the counseling broke down and her hopes for help felt lost, her despair deepened. She felt like a failure and left in tears; however, the counselor followed her out, took her aside, looked into her eyes and said, "It is not your fault." Those words of truth gave her life and the courage to go on at a critical and emotional moment.

The movie "The Blind Side" tells the true story of Leigh Anne and Sean Tuohy and their children, whose words backed up by action made a huge difference in the life of a young man, Michael Ohre. Through their love, acceptance, and encouragement, and also that of some teachers, he reached beyond his circumstances and was awarded a football scholarship. His high school coach, who was at first disappointed with his performance, quickly learned Michael's best response was from receiving encouraging words and acceptance. This encouragement allowed his talent to flourish which led to his success and hence being sought after by many collegiate teams. Michael Ohre completed his football college scholarship with many honors and was later drafted by the NFL's Baltimore Ravens.

One of the most influential people I have ever met is Pastor John. Beyond dedicating his life to teaching the truth from God's word, he encourages people at every opportunity. He spends time meeting with and listening to people, encouraging them to follow their dreams of reaching out to others. Often he becomes their advocate helping them make connections along the way. Pastor John also takes time to encourage hundreds of people with personal letters or notes. There have been over thirty people who have taken on a full time life of serving others, due in part to his encouragement. Truthful words of encouragement have power!

> From the fruit of their speech people are well
> satisfied; their work results in reward.
> Proverbs 12:14 (CEB)

Group Discussion:

1. It is easy to "bend" the truth. Have you ever thought, *I did not report that accurately,* or *I exaggerated*? Why do we find it so hard to tell the truth accurately?

2. Have you ever assumed you understood someone and later realized you had it all wrong? Give an example of a recent misunderstanding.

3. Were your parents encouragers or discouragers? How might this affect your parenting style?

4. Share a time when someone's words had a big impact on you for good or for bad.

5. Share a time you took action or continued on because of someone's encouraging words.

6. Do you believe that words have the power of life and death? Can you give an example?

7. Why is it important not to take offense and to pray about our reaction to hurtful words?

8. Why do our words mirror or reflect our heart? Do you think this reflection could be distorted?

9. In what arena of your life would you like to improve your communication?

Our Work Matters

This day will come only once,
Time dispersed, soon the sun will set.
Will I smile at today and the difference it made,
Or look back and wish with regret?

Whatever you do, work at it with all your heart, as
working for the Lord, not for men, since you know
that you will receive an inheritance from the Lord as
a reward. Colossians 3:23–24 (NIV, © 1985)

ithout work, lasting satisfaction and reward is a
mirage. Though many of us wish we never had to
work another day in our lives, in reality we know
not working, "doesn't work"! Our personal and communal survival
depends on it. Beyond the paycheck, work gives us a sense of
accomplishment, self-respect, and plays a role in our happiness.
The work we choose, whether we are paid or not, is an expression
of what we value. Loving what we do, and/or the people we do it

for, greatly enriches our lives and helps us to get up each morning. Thinking positively about our work affects our overall performance and happiness. Taking the time to identify and prioritize what is most important and the people and tasks involved, helps us to keep a balance in life. Otherwise, before we realize it, we don't have time for what is most important to us. God has created us with a purpose and he will use our work to refine us and impact the lives of others. How we choose to use our time, day in and day out, will affect our emotions, relationships, and quality of life.

We have a diverse and intricate world with millions of jobs that need to be done. Which of these jobs were designed to be done by you? Does your present work fit your personality, gifts, and temperament? Consider your life goals and what you value. Take time to talk to people in the fields you are drawn to and get advice from people who know you well (Proverbs 19:20). Pray for God to guide your heart as you seek your purpose (Proverbs 19:21). Ask God to direct you and to provide the training and preparation you need along the way. Together with him follow your dream as it evolves and becomes God's call! Choosing wisely has the potential to impact your family, the community you live in, and God's plan for our world. God desires to guide you and work alongside you in whatever you do. He wants to develop a passion within you that will provide motivation, perseverance, and satisfaction. Taking time to evaluate with a thankful attitude is profitable. If you are working in a job which conflicts with your personality or values, look to God for redirection. Seek out people who can advise you and make a plan to get the knowledge and skills you need to make a change. Be bold if you believe God wants to move you. Ultimately God is our provider, so when he calls us to something new he also provides a way for us to follow him. Every job that needs to be done is important, especially when we work with an attitude of pleasing God, who is our source for contentment and reward. Be patient in the process of finding God's best for your life, because it is often a part of God's plan to prepare us. God has work he has planned for you and people he is planning for you to help along the way, by your knowledge, skills, encouragement, and example.

We all know doing a good job at work or school is important to our reputation, as well as our future. It is essential for our own contentment and in gaining the respect of others. Doing our best also has an effect on the community around us. Consider the ripple effect that your job, when done well, has on the lives of others. When we put into practice God's loving principles, we become better at our jobs. Most of us do our jobs in the context of relationships, so encouraging the people with whom we work or go to school goes a long way in bringing positive results on both a personal and organizational level. Relying on God to discern the truth, particularly in difficult circumstances, will help us make wise decisions. Loving the people around us by looking to their needs, as well as our own, improves our work or learning environment. Virtually every one of God's principles also applies to the workplace, such as the way we use our words, being positive yet truthful, showing we care, doing our best, and trusting God with the things that are not in our control. Even applying the principles for fighting evil has an effect on our work. Imagine the benefits for your business, school, or place of work. How do clients react when we show our respect and engage by listening? If we genuinely put their needs as the bottom line, would they happily recommend us or our business to others? Would they be more likely to trust us as civil servants and leaders? God knows each of us and every angle of a situation. We can never go wrong following God's precepts and trusting him for the outcome. God promises to ultimately bless us when we are working and living for others.

Showing we care about the people we work with every day, instead of complaining or being indifferent will bring fulfilment to our life and influence theirs (Philippians 2:14–16). It is important that we set our mind to it. If we are working in a negative environment we need God's help to be patient and stay positive. Our caring attitude and our prayers have the power to bring a positive change to a negative culture. We can make an impact if we tune in to the needs around us, on a professional level and at times on a personal level. Be sensitive to social boundaries; for example, it may not be appropriate to ask about personal issues or pray for someone in a public place. If you sense someone is hurting when you greet them, get away at lunch break or someplace private to get into a deeper discussion. Be a listening ear if they want one, or discover if you could meet a need. Some of you may be thinking, '*I know an attractive woman or someone tall, dark and handsome I would love to reach out to*'. If you are married, or they are, be very, very careful!! If you feel they could use encouragement or some help, find someone of the same sex who can reach out to them, so that neither of you is led into a temptation which could ultimately destroy your life. There is nothing more attractive then someone who cares! There is evil seeking to destroy lives, so don't set yourself up.

Perseverance is also an important quality at school or in the workplace; a principle we will discuss further in chapter nine. Getting up each day, even when we feel like sleeping in, takes effort. Showing grace with people when we are just fed up is perseverance.

Having to rely on God to get our attitude right again, day after day, takes consistency. To complete a job well usually takes time, energy, and persistence. It is an effort to keep our mind and body engaged until our task is complete. Developing perseverance is an important part of building our character and loving people. Staying focused on our goals and relationships over time will bring us satisfaction and joy. To enable us to go the course, God designed for us to have a day of rest. Set aside at least one day a week to enjoy him, his creation, and each other. Get together with other believers to sing with joy, share each other's lives, and be encouraged. Without it we will become physically and spiritually bankrupt. Take your day of rest and be renewed!

Not only should we take a day of rest each week, but we need to keep a healthy balance in our active lives! On a regular basis we need time alone with God. Friends and families need time to enjoy each other. Taking time to enjoy the beauty of our world and the wonder of nature gives us a glimpse of God's majesty. Enjoying the life of a city sparks our imaginations. The pleasure of time with each other around a dinner table bonds our relationships. "I know that there is nothing better for people than to be happy and to do good while they live. That each of them may eat and drink, and find satisfaction in all their toil—this is the gift of God" (Ecclesiastes 3:13). Satisfaction in our work, time with friends and family, and taking time to do good for others is all part of a healthy balance. A strong relationship with God, giving us faith to believe his promises even when he calls us to persevere, helps us to stay balanced. Jesus impressed on us that our "work" is to believe (John 6:29). Allowing God to guide our life work demonstrates our belief. Our belief, our faith, is proven to be real by our actions, doing God's work of loving others as he guides us (James 2:14–26). Spending time with God and responding to his guidance enables us to have satisfaction in all our work and relationships. It is the key to a balanced life and finding the love and contentment we are searching for.

If we are willing to do our best and care for others as God asks of us, it cannot help but make a positive difference, in both our work and workplace. People will see the joy in us that flows from God. They will see our caring attitude and honesty. They will see the respect we show authority and the grace we give to those around us. When we are kind in the face of opposition people will notice. Good character and perseverance will have a positive effect. Co-workers will be attracted to your positive attitude and strong relationships. God is pursuing the people you work with, drawing them toward himself and he is using you! As they are drawn, be ready to invite them to your home and church, to become part of a caring community. Our evolving character of increasing love and grace paints a picture and our purposeful work is a canvas that displays God's masterpiece. As those around us interpret the paintings of our lives, we have a chance to share our story—the story of how God has changed us. As we make the decision, day by day, to allow God to be the painter, our transformation becomes a part of reaching out and living for love!

What do workers gain from their toil? I have seen the burden God has laid on the human race. He has made everything beautiful in its time. He has also set eternity in the human heart; yet no one can fathom what God has done from beginning to end. I know that there is nothing better for people than to be happy and to do good while they live. That each of them may eat and drink, and find satisfaction in all their toil—this is the gift of God. Ecclesiastes 3:9–13

For it is God who works in you to will and to act according to his good purpose. Do everything without complaining or arguing, so that you might become blameless and pure, children of God without fault in a crooked and depraved generation, in which you shine like stars in the universe as you hold out the word of life... Philippians 2:13–16a (NIV, © 1985)

And in fact you love all of God's family... Yet we urge you brothers and sisters, to do more and more, and to make it your ambition to lead a quiet life: You should mind your own business [no gossip] and work with your hands, just as we told you, so that your daily life may win the respect of outsiders and so that you may not be dependent on anybody. 1 Thessalonians 4:10–12

Do nothing out of selfish ambition or vain conceit. Rather, in humility value others above yourselves, not looking to your own interests but each of you to the interest of others. Philippians 2:4

For it is by grace you have been saved, through faith—and this is not from yourselves it is the gift of God—not by works, so that no one can boast. For we are God's handiwork, created in Jesus Christ to do good works, which God prepared in advance for us to do. Ephesians 2:8–10

The Reading Teacher

Grace works long hours teaching children to read at an elementary school which serves many families in poverty. To teach a child to read requires extra patience and encouragement. Her sister did not have a nine-to-five job and was a stay at home mom for many years, having time to volunteer in the church and community. Sometimes, Grace would begin to feel guilty and ask her sister, "You're always volunteering. What should I do?" Couldn't she see her whole life is reaching out in love? God has directed her path of service, as she truly pours her life into the children, many of whom have difficult home lives. Grace has a deep commitment, working hard to encourage the students and holding children accountable to do the work required for success. Though it would often be easier to let some students slide, she works to spend the extra time with students who need it, or who have no one to help them. She loves the children and she knows that without learning to read their success will be limited. Grace has a compassionate heart and at times she reaches out to her students' families. She is also supportive of her co-workers on both a professional and personal level. The demand of doing the job well uses most of her energy, yet she still has a family and home to look after and is the first to call a friend or family member in need. Taking the time she needs to rest is crucial to enable her to have the patience she needs each day to do her job well. Not only is she teaching struggling students to read, she impacts children, parents, and co-workers as they see Jesus through her life. God gave Grace a big heart and a desire to help children, and then led her to work that was meant for her!

Group Discussion:

1. Share with each other what type of work you currently do and whether you are content in your job.
2. Do you feel your life has a healthy balance between work, home, and other activities? If not, where would you make changes?
3. Are there people at work or school who make your day go better? Why?
4. Have there been aspects of your work or dealing with difficulty in your job that have helped you grow as a person? How?
5. Choose one of God's principles that we have discussed over the course of our study and give an example of how it could affect your home, school, or workplace.
6. Why may who you are, rather than what you do in your job, have a bigger effect on the people you come in contact with?
7. If you could pick any job, what would it be and why? Have you explored avenues to make a change?
8. Do you think God has created you for a particular job? Why or why not?

CHAPTER 8

Sharing our Lives as We Share the Good News

Time, I shared mine and listened,
I heard the beat of a heart.
The dream that was dashed...
"Hope of tomorrow, what if they need a new start?"

I know disappointment and anger,
To be sad, insecure, and alone.
My journey created my story,
"Help me share how I find my way home."

But in your hearts revere Christ as Lord. Always be
prepared to give an answer to anyone who asks you
to give the reason for the hope that you have. But do
this with gentleness and respect... 1 Peter 3:15

haring our lives is the perfect way to share the good news of Jesus in a context that is open and real. Being willing to be ourselves, share our struggles, and show concern for others makes all the difference. When we treat people with respect and take a genuine interest in their lives, it opens the door. Sharing hospitality develops friendships, bringing joy and laughter to our lives. We learn more about God as we open up and seek him together, developing confidence and a supportive community. Sharing our story—how God showed up in *our* lives—helps others be receptive to the truth that God is real and active in the lives of men and women. God teaches us how to love as we step out and interact with people. The world longs to hear a story of hope!

People are attracted to people who are full of life. When we respond to the prompting of the Spirit of truth people will see life in us as our identity is linked with God's love. Our lives help to correct misconceptions people have about following God if we are willing to be ourselves and resist putting on an act. When we share our ups and downs, our struggles, victories, and failures people can identify with our story. We can relate how God transformed our self-worth and our relationships as we realized God's true love for us. Others will see how God gives us purpose, identity, and contentment. Some will wonder about our security, seeing that God is the rock we hold on to when times are tough.

Everyone enjoys someone who is genuinely interested in their lives—their thoughts, ideas, problems, and future. We reflect God's character when we take our minds off ourselves and focus on the people we are with. Jesus observed the people around him and asked questions to draw them out. Asking questions helps us develop relationships and also keeps the conversation flowing. Having a few questions in mind can help us feel comfortable when we are meeting someone new. Listen carefully and share your own life experiences, good or bad, especially as they relate to what *he* or *she* is sharing. Giving our time and showing a sincere interest builds friendships and trust. An opportunity to share about our relationship with God will likely arise, as he becomes a big part of our lives and who we turn to with our problems. First Peter tells us to be prepared. "But in your hearts set apart Christ as Lord. Always be prepared to give an answer to anyone who asks you to give the reason for the hope that you have. But do this with gentleness and respect..." (1 Peter 3:15, NIV © 1965). Notice how it starts, deciding that the work of God is a priority in your day—"But in your hearts set apart Christ as Lord." God is in charge and there is nothing more important to him than people. When the Spirit of truth whispers, that sets my priority. It goes on to say we need to be prepared to give the reason for our hope—to be able to express to others the good news of Jesus and our own story of what God has done in our lives, so that when someone asks we can speak boldly with gentleness. The exercises and questions in this chapter will help you prepare. First Peter 3 also assures us that most of the time good will come from our kindness, encouragement, and message, but even if it doesn't God promises to bless us.

"Do this with gentleness and respect." It is important to be careful in the way we speak to others. We never want to be argumentative or judgmental of their lifestyles or beliefs; instead always treat people with respect. We are not approving sin by treating people with respect and kindness, but rather seeing from the perspective that we all fall short (Romans 3:23). We all grow in our beliefs; no one is exempt from the process of learning about truth. By showing people respect we open up the opportunity to share the key for recognizing and overcoming the sin and false beliefs that steal from our lives. We should consider the culture and context around us and stay within healthy social boundaries. Communicate in an open and gentle way, guiding others to a realization of God's concern and provision for their lives. By giving people our time, listening, and sharing our own experience and the good news of Jesus as the Spirit leads, we can guide people to a realization of God's love and companionship.

Following are some practical ways to prepare ourselves to share the gospel—the good news the Bible teaches us about Jesus. Find the one that is the most natural to you by practicing. Preparing as a group activity builds confidence as we practice sharing our stories with each other. Then, when we sense the Holy Spirit is asking us to speak, we are prepared and feel more comfortable. God is right there with us to help!

One way to share God's plan is to draw a diagram of a canyon, showing how we were separated from God because of our sin. Then draw the cross which represents Jesus, and his death and resurrection to pay for sin, thus providing us a bridge to God and eternal life. This picture lesson is a memorable and a simple way to share the gospel. Below is a simplified diagram from Navigators. God has made a way to end our separation; *He* crossed over and rescued us from evil and death. Will we trust Jesus enough to walk with him, trusting his death and resurrection as our bridge to life? We can have a relationship with God, who created us and loves us beyond our comprehension! We can become part of his family and live with him forever.

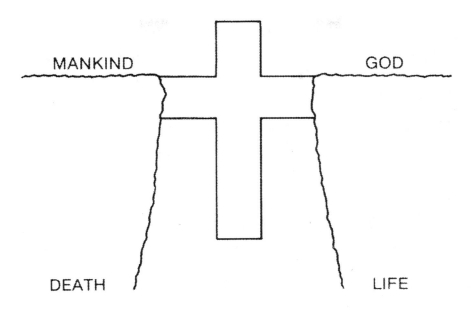

The Bible explains God's plan to bring us into an eternal relationship with him as his children. Look for a Bible translation with language you can understand, relate to, and share. Look up the following verses and pray for God to reveal his great plan of love to you in a renewed way that will give you a passion to share it with others as the Spirit of truth provides opportunities. Tell how Jesus defeated death and the control of sin on our lives in order to save us and how we can experience his love.

Luke 1   John 1:1–18, 29–34   John 3 John 11:25–30
John 12:44–50   John 14:6, 23–27
The Crucifixion: John 19   The Resurrection: John 20
Peters address: Acts 2:14–41
Romans 3:21–26   Colossians 1:15–23   1 John 1:5–10
1 John 4:7–21   1 John 5: 11–12, 18–20

Write out a few of your favorite verses from the readings and try to memorize at least one. From there God will help you develop your own way to share God's truths, as it suits each situation.

The four spiritual principles (adapted from Cru) **are another way to share the good news.** See Cru's presentation at cru.org/how-to-know-god/would-you-like-to-know-god-personally.

1. <u>God loves us and has a wonderful plan for our life.</u> Read John 3:16–17 and Jeremiah 29:11. God created us and loves us. He has a purpose and plan for each of us. The Bible is full of ordinary men and women whom God enabled to care for his people and to take part in his plan for our world.

2. <u>Man is sinful and separated from God.</u> Therefore we cannot experience God's love or know God's plan for our life without his intervention. Read Romans 3:23–25 and 6:23. Spiritual death is separation from God and this separation is eternal and frightening. We need God! He cannot comfort and direct us in a close relational way if we remain in our unrepentant sinful state. He is perfectly good and just and we are not!

3. <u>Jesus Christ is God's only provision for man's sin. Through him we can know and experience God's love and plan for our life.</u> Read Romans 5:6–10, John 3:16–18, 14:6, and 1 Corinthians 15:3–6. God loved us so much he was willing to go through death on a cross, in order that our relationship to him would be restored. Jesus overcame death, breaking the power of sin and ending our separation. Now God, through

the Holy Spirit of truth, can comfort, help, and give us purpose we could never know on our own.

4. <u>We must receive Jesus Christ individually as our Savior and Lord; then we can know and experience God's love and plan for our lives.</u> Read John 1:12 and Ephesians 2:8–9. He is our Savior because he saves us from our sin that separates us from him. He is our Lord because he has authority to direct us. If we are willing to follow, God will give us purpose and a plan for our lives. This plan usually involves our natural talents and spiritual gifts. After all he made us! He knows us better than anyone, better than we know ourselves, and has set us in a time and place in history for a purpose.

Sharing our Story

Often the Holy Spirit invites you to share your own story. For some people this comes quite naturally, but for others it takes time and practice. On the following page there is a guide you can copy to help you write out your story and practice it. As long as you are moving forward with God, he is able to use you! "For God did not give us a spirit of timidity, but a spirit of power, of love, and of self-discipline. So do not be ashamed to testify about our Lord…" (2 Timothy 1:7)

SHARE YOUR STORY

"You are my witnesses," declares the Lord,

"and my servant whom I have chosen, so that you may know and believe me and understand that I am he. Before me no god was formed, nor will there be one after me.

I, even I, am the Lord and apart from me there is no savior." Isaiah 43:10–11

Changed lives are the evidence of God's love. Answer these questions to help you verbalize your testimony.

Everyone has a story to tell.

Who did I understand God to be, at first?

How do I know God is real? How or when did God reveal to me new insights of who He was?

Who was I before I trusted Jesus? Consider past thoughts, desires, relationships and actions.

What happened that lead me to trust Jesus?

What has changed for me, in me, and in my relationships since I have trusted Christ?

When have I felt God's presence in a time of need? What other significant events played a role in your story?

Write out and practice sharing your experience. How has God affected your life? Use some of the answers above to help. God asks us to share what we have learned about him; especially who he is to us personally!

Hospitality

We have greater opportunity to share our stories when we share our lives. Hospitality is a wonderful way to do that. People love to get together to enjoy some food, laughter, music, and conversation. Be the person at your work or in your neighborhood who gets people together for a good time. Some people have a real gift for hosting and making others feel comfortable, but we can all learn tips from an array of sources to help us enjoy entertaining. If it is a spur of the moment invitation, great—just relax and go with the flow. Otherwise preparing a relaxing atmosphere and some of the food ahead of time allows us to enjoy our guests once they arrive. Pray beforehand that everyone will delight in their time together. Then just be yourself and relax, enjoying the music, food, and each other. If you are having a good time your guests will too!

Grow Together

Another effective way to build relationships is to ask your friends and neighbors to a Bible study. You will be surprised at how many would like to come. Perhaps you have never studied the Bible. Why not start with a group of friends or neighbors? *Starting Point: Find Your Place in the Story* by Andy Stanley is a good example of a beginning study which has a DVD available to make it easy. Many Bible studies have a video presentation and discussion questions to take the pressure off you. Choosing a book of the Bible or the parables and teachings of Jesus, reading and discussing what you learn or can put into action in your everyday life is also a great option. There are many helpful study Bibles and resources available that are easy to use. If you have found this book helpful, but read it on your own, consider going through it with a group to help others find their path on their journey with God. As a group we grow together as we interact in our communication and relationships. Make meetings fun and help people relax by adding lunch or dinner, everyone bringing a dish to share, or perhaps just take turns bringing appetizers or dessert. If you are not comfortable in a group setting, another option is meeting one on one with a friend, neighbor, or workmate. Our lives are enriched as we discover and enjoy new relationships and a closer walk with God.

Celebrate Baptism

As our family, friends, and neighbors discover their own relationship with Jesus and become a part of God's family, take time to celebrate baptism. New believers can be baptized at a local church, pool, river, lake, or even in the ocean. They identify with Jesus in his death as they are dunked under the water and with him in his resurrection as they rise up from the water. A beautiful picture of new life we can share together with family and friends. (Matthew 28:19-20, 1 Peter 3:21-22, Colossians 2:9-12, Acts 16:31-34 and Acts 22:15-16)

A Rainbow of Love

My husband and I had the privilege of living a few years in Argentina. During our time there we hosted the study, *Starting Point: Find Your Place in the Story* for internationals that lived in the city. We enjoyed food, laughter, and each other as we discovered more about God and developed a supportive community. There was a young woman from China who attended and we soon learned she was living on the street during the day, but had a position where she stayed at night to care for an elderly woman. She had to hang out at coffee shops or internet cafes when she was not working.

Inviting Li Qin to share her story, she told of her father who had been very stern with her as she was growing up. Eventually he had driven her away. Li Qin had learned he was dying alone in China, so she sublet her apartment to have the money to bring him to Argentina and be beside him as he died. Now he was gone and she was alone with no place to stay for a year. We gave her a key to our apartment so she could come and go, having a place to wash and rest. Soon we started to study the Bible together. Having had a stern father, Li Qin saw God in the same way. God's true character began to shine through his word, and it was a delight to see her face light up as she learned of the great love God had for her. One day, as she was reading the story of Noah in the book of Genesis about the covenant rainbow God gave as a promise of his love for us, she looked up and there it was. A perfect rainbow—God's watercolor painted across the sky beyond our big glass window. Amazed, Li Qin realized it was a sign of God's love for her, a personal promise that he would always care for her. She gave her life to Jesus, finally believing it was all true! She experienced God's love and I had the great joy of being a part of it. We both experienced the truth of God's promises as we shared our lives and our stories.

Group Discussion:

1. Have you ever had a misconception about God that someone helped you to correct? How?
2. Have you ever shared a story about yourself to encourage someone?
3. Why is it important to be deliberate and intentional with our lives, if we want to show others God's love?
4. Share the verse you memorized or the method of sharing the Gospel that you found most comfortable.

Group Activity:

Use the "Share Your Story" worksheet to help you articulate what God has done in your life. Plan a time for each of you to practice sharing your story out loud. This will help you to overcome any insecurity you may feel about speaking to others. Sharing feels more natural once we prepare. Your story can make a difference for someone else.

9

Perseverance

Like a tulip in spring, our passion broke through.
Like a rose in the summer, sweet purpose grew.
So weary by autumn, yet the harvest is near,
On through the winter, *"Help us trust and persevere!"*
A new spring is coming and hope will prevail.
God's promise to us—"Love never fails!"

Let us not become weary in doing good,
for at the proper time we will reap a harvest
if we do not give up. Galatians 6:9

Seeing God use us in the lives of others is satisfying! We feel blessed and grateful as we experience God's hand guiding us. But, what is energizing at first may after time become exhausting, and even overwhelming. There is a spiritual battle going on that we cannot see, although we can see the effects and often feel it. It is so important to rely, moment by moment, on God and not give up. If God gives you a task, mission, or calling and you have moved forward in faith, do not let doubt and weariness stop you from fighting the good fight until God has completed his work through you. Looking for the positive and giving thanks, in the face of life's difficulties, has power. Perseverance brings great blessing!

People often make the mistake of thinking that if God gives us a task, he will pave the way so that everything goes smoothly, but that is not biblical. Read chapter eleven in Hebrews about all the great men and women in Old Testament history who took action in faith. At the end of the Chapter we read, "These were all commended for their faith, yet none of them received what had been promised." Wow, it did not work out for any of them as they expected! We know God did fulfill his promises to them, but not until after their life on earth had ended. For example, we know that Abraham did become the father of many nations, even though he did not have his first child until he was eighty-six years old and his second at age one-hundred (Genesis 16:16, 17:18–20, 21:5, 22:17–18, Romans 4:16–17). Hebrews goes on to say, "God had planned something better for us so that only together with us would they be made perfect" (Hebrews 11:40). Would we say that Abraham or Moses were not successful in God's eyes? Of course not! God was pleased, even though they each had moments they would not be proud of. They needed the redemption Christ accomplished applied to their lives, just as we do. But as we take a look at their lives in the Old Testament we can see a process of going forward in faith time and time again. These men and women of faith kept believing, no matter the circumstances, and kept acting on that belief. They talked to God when they had doubts, expecting and waiting for his response, instead of turning from him. We also need to go forward in faith, talk to God, learn from our mistakes, and go forward again, relying on God all the more! We need to look to God to direct us and trust God for the outcome. This kind of perseverance changes our character; we become more like Jesus. This is the process of sanctification—becoming more and more people of good character whom God can use—people who listen to the Spirit of truth and put God's purposes first and who are filled with God's grace and love. For all of us, no matter where our lives fall in history, we are not yet the holy people God promises we will be in the future.

You could put it like this: We all need some pruning! Pruning is good! Jesus said, "I am the true vine and my father is the gardener. He cuts off every branch in me that bears no fruit, while every branch that does bear fruit he prunes so that it will be even more fruitful." He goes on to say, "I am the vine; you are the branches. If a man remains in me and I in him, he will bear much fruit; apart from me he can do nothing" (John 15:1–17). The bottom line is that we can do absolutely nothing of lasting value without God (Actually we need him to take our next breath, since he is the sustainer of life). We must allow God to make changes in our lives, to prune us and remove the dead branches from our lives, so we can grow in character and become fruitful in loving others. We need Jesus interceding on our behalf; we need the person of the Holy Spirit to guide us, step by step, for our lives to make a lasting difference in our world. Things are not always going to go smoothly, which should be no surprise. Trials in which we persevere by faith are often what God uses to do the pruning, so he can make us better people. Outreach and loving others is not exempt from this, but rather some of the richest soil where some of the most fruitful pruning can be done. Some people give up and become bitter or disillusioned, but others turn to God, persevere, and become the most mature, beautiful, and loving people.

Commitment is the first step toward perseverance. I once heard a missionary to Africa say he was getting too old for other people's good ideas. On a trip home to the United States he was addressing the lack of commitment he saw in the church. If you have the idea, God is usually calling you to spearhead the effort. He is inviting you to join him in his work. You need to commit! Do not let anything get in the way if God is calling you to fill a role of service in the church or to reach out within your community. Don't let anything derail you if you know God is calling you to a faraway place where there are people in darkness and need. It may take time and planning, but commit to move forward step by step, allowing God to lead the way. Whether a life mission or something as simple as meeting with a co-worker for lunch on a regular basis to forge a relationship, if you do not commit, other things get in the way. Nothing is more important to you and your family than being in the center of God's will. Perseverance and commitment help to keep you there!

As we can see from Hebrews 11, sometimes our hope is not fulfilled in our lifetime. What do the lives of our most prominent historical figures have in common, such as Abraham Lincoln and Martin Luther King, Jr.? They had an unshakable belief in a God-given idea or principle and perseverance within their own lives that was above and beyond. These are the lives that make great strides for humankind! Another such man was William Carey.

Amazing Perseverance

William Carey, a poor English shoemaker, believed with all his heart that all of the world should be able to have the Bible in their language. He passionately believed those living in Asia should have the opportunity to know Jesus loved them personally and set his life course to that end, though the task seemed impossible and he met constant resistance. Carey trained to become a pastor, inspired others, set sail twice (the first time he was delayed), and lived fourty years working in India. He buried a five year old son and two wives, the second a blessing in his work, but the first a woman overwhelmed by the life he had chosen. Throughout all his trials he remained patient and gentle with people. Even after working long days in a factory in order to provide for his family, he worked tirelessly to translate the Bible, set up schools, and teach. Eventually, he translated the whole Bible in three different dialects and also contributed to other translations; work that in itself takes amazing perseverance! In a warehouse fire in 1812 his manuscripts were destroyed, which he took very hard, but determinedly translated them again! He made an impact on India, not only by translating God's word, but also fighting against such practices as widow burning. He called us to be responsible for the fate of others and took up the call himself. Though he may often have felt like a failure in his early life, his life sparked a movement in history, which in turn has enabled today's Asian nationals to take up the cause that he and many others lived and died for. Their perseverance is even now taking root in the lives of others; they were ordinary people who lived extraordinary lives! (Story adapted from Ruth Ann Tucker's book, *From Jerusalem to Irian Jaya*)

Another story of a lifetime of perseverance is the life of my good friend, Brenda. Brenda and her husband were both called to go to China to share God's love and the good news of Jesus at a young age. They married and set out with idealistic dreams. Time after time they met discouragement as health problems brought them out of China. One time Brenda's husband was taken by medivac helicopter! He had developed severe asthma due to China's poor air quality and the damp conditions where mold could easily grow. Brenda was left inland with her two small children not knowing the fate of her protector. Still they stayed faithful in their call, eventually all moving to Hong Kong for better air quality. During these years Brenda had developed a passion for the orphan children of China and wanted with all her heart to make a difference. She persevered taking whatever chance she could to cross back into China and spend a day loving children. She always showed great respect for the workers even as she gently suggested changes and found donors for better equipment. I know she often felt frustrated that she could not care for the children personally, but God was watching and had plans for her. He saw her heart and her perseverance.

In 2004 there was a devastating earthquake and tsunami in Asia. The Hong Kong church gave much to help with the disaster relief and Brenda was asked to go to India to assess how the donations had been used. During her time there some national Indian workers challenged her to oversee establishing a home for children who had been affected by the tsunami and severe poverty in a coastal city. As a couple, they took on the challenge and two years later moved to India to work alongside the national workers. For years they were like a mom and dad to about twenty-six children whom they loved and taught. They personally helped to educate the children and when that was no longer possible they made arrangements for further education. By seeking donations they plan to see as many as possible through college, which is a miracle for children in their situation, in part because they are from the lowest caste in India. These children are bright, creative, loving, and now have hope. Brenda and her family's perseverance have blessed the children's lives, giving them a fighting chance, both as individuals and collectively as they make a difference in their community. They will be the leaders of the future!

> Therefore, since we are surrounded by such a great cloud of witnesses, let us throw off everything that hinders and the sin that so easily entangles. And let us run with perseverance the race marked out for us, fixing our eyes on Jesus, the pioneer and perfecter of our faith. For the joy set before him he endured the cross, scorning its shame, and sat down at the right hand of the throne of God. Consider him who endured such opposition from sinners, so that you will not grow weary and lose heart. Hebrews 12:1–3

> For everything that was written in the past was written to teach us, so that through the endurance taught in the Scriptures and the encouragement they provide we might have hope. May the God who gives endurance and encouragement give you the same attitude of mind toward each other that Christ Jesus had, so that with one mind and one voice you may glorify the God and Father of our Lord Jesus Christ. Accept one another, then, just as Christ accepted you, in order to bring praise to God. Romans 15:4–7

We continually ask God to fill you with the knowledge of his will through all the wisdom and understanding that the Spirit gives, so that you might live a life worthy of the Lord and please him in every way: bearing fruit in every good work, growing in the knowledge of God, being strengthened with all his power according to his glorious might so that you may have great endurance and patience, and giving joyful thanks to the Father, who has qualified you to share in the inheritance of his holy people in the kingdom of light.
Colossians 1:9b–12

Group Discussion:

1. Have you ever experienced having things *not* go the way you planned when you set out to do something good? Please share your experience. How did you react and what were the results?

2. Did you turn to God as you faced the set-back? Why or why not and did it make a difference?

3. Share a situation in which God used a trial in your life to develop your character.

4. Has God ever pruned something from your life that helped you "bear fruit"?

5. Tell us about a time when, by learning from the past, you were better prepared for a new opportunity.

6. Read Romans 15:1–13. Why is perseverance often related to our relationships? Who are the Gentiles and who is the Root of Jesse? What two groups are being encouraged to accept each other and by what power?

7. Do you know of anyone you admire for their perseverance? Do they inspire you and how?

CHAPTER 10

Seasons

A child longs to be older. *Then I can...*
A teen longs to be independent. *Then I can...*
A university student longs for a job. *Then I can...*
A parent longs for some rest. *Then I can...*
A worker longs for retirement. *Then I can...*
A grey haired man longs to be young again. *If only I could...*

> There is a time for everything, and a season for every activity under the heavens: ... Ecclesiastes 3:1

G od has designed our life upon this earth in seasons. From birth to death we go through different stages, each with its own set of joys and responsibilities. Solomon, a great king, the son of King David, was blessed with both wisdom and riches, yet asks in the beautiful book of Ecclesiastes, "What does it all mean? Will my fortune or wisdom help me in the end? Am I any happier than those who work for me? What accomplishments are important?" Each season of our life we face new joys, new challenges, and new opportunities to reach out and love others. Will we make the most of our life, seeking to know God with our eyes open to the people around us day by day? Embracing each season of our life will help us to be content and to make the most of them. In this last chapter let's consider the seasons of our lives as they relate to loving and serving others. Being thankful for and enjoying every stage of life will help us be content along the way. Each season has new opportunities to grow in our relationships, enabling us to finish well and hear the words of Jesus as we pass into eternal life, "Well done, good and faithful servant! ... Come share your master's happiness!" (Matthew 25:21)

Childhood and Parenting

Childhood can be both full of wonder and full of disillusionment. Children look at the world with idealistic eyes of faith, but are too often disappointed by the harsh reality of the world. We can help children keep their beautiful faith by being more like Jesus with them, always happy to listen, giving our love and protection. Parents have a great influence in this season of life. Children watch and imitate, and whether good or bad, thankful or angry, parents' lives play a significant part in how they develop and what choices they make. However, even bad parenting can motivate children to do good, if they have someone to point them to God. Kindness to a child in a tough home situation can help them to see the love of God, giving them hope and a desire to be different. Childhood is when our first choices are made. Teaching children that God cares about them and has made rules for their well-being will help them make good choices. Learning obedience often comes with making mistakes. Learning to turn to God, and also each other, to ask forgiveness is essential for a successful life. We can set an example if we openly ask forgiveness for our mistakes.

Valuing people is something we can begin to learn at a young age. If you have children, take the step of reaching out to their friends and classmates. When possible, be active in your children's activities and invite their friends to your home. Seeing that we care for the people we come in contact with teaches our children to value relationships. If a child expresses interest in helping someone, encourage and support them. Our help enables them to put their good thoughts into action. Assist children's God given imagination, giving them opportunities to explore and implement some of their ideas. As they become teens, their independence and character are developed as we encourage them to develop their ideas and take responsibility to plan, implement, and follow through. They will learn by experience to listen and trust God as they go forward.

If you love children, but cannot have your own, the age of childbearing can be a painful time of life. Be assured God cares deeply. Consider that he may be drawing you to play a bigger role in the lives of children, a role you would have a hard time filling if you were caring for your own children. Or God may possibly have in mind a lonely child that he wants to match with you. He knows your family would be just what he or she needs. He wants to turn your sorrow into happiness. *May God give you the joy you are looking for and show you his plan for fulfillment.*

But Jesus called the children to him and said, "Let the little children come to me, and do not hinder them, for the kingdom of God belongs to such as these. Truly I tell you, anyone who will not receive the kingdom of God like a little child will never enter it." Luke 18:16–17

Fix these words of mine in your hearts and minds; ...Teach them to your children, talking about them when you sit at home and when you walk along the road, when you lie down and when you get up. Deut. 11:18–19

Don't let anyone look down on you because you are young, but set an example for the believers, in speech, in conduct, in love, in faith and in purity. 1 Timothy 4:12

Young Adults

As young adults we emerge to take on our own identity. It is a time when our world is expanded and our world view changes as we venture out of the environment in which we've grown up. Taking advantage of opportunities to learn about other people's ideas and cultures is an important part of this process and will broaden our perspective. If you have never had the opportunity to travel overseas or experience firsthand a culture that is not your own, this is a great time to do it. Consider a student exchange or missions trip. If the expense would ordinarily hold you back, you can be creative in finding donors and prayer partners; involving others enables each of you to impact lives. Whether home or abroad, being involved in outreach to others will enrich your life and help you set good priorities for the future.

In our late teens and twenties some of our biggest decisions are made, such as choosing our career, work, or trade which we have previously explored. That choice may lead to a life lived in service to others such as a profession in the medical field, social justice, social work, teacher, or missionary. However, a life of service and caring is possible in whatever field we choose with God's guidance. God may call some to be stay-at-home parents, investing in the lives of the leaders of tomorrow. Seeking God and his will for our lives is what matters. We have all heard of people who choose careers aimed to serve, but become corrupt and end up doing more harm than good. As young adults set a course of integrity! It is a time in our lives when we are choosing our priorities. Choose to live for God and his people and enjoy life along the way!

One of the most crucial life decisions we make, usually as a young adult, is who we marry. When it comes to fulfilling our dreams and purpose in life, choosing our lifetime partner will have a profound effect. Decide ahead of time what boundaries you will set in dating so that attraction does not override your principles. As you date, discuss your hopes and dreams. Do they match up; are they listening? Do you desire to love God with all your heart, mind, and strength and make it a priority to love others? Be sure your future husband or wife has the same guiding purpose. The most satisfying marriages begin with mutual respect and a desire to see one another's dreams fulfilled. If you feel God is revealing to you a mission or purpose for your life consider how that aligns with their hopes and dreams. Remember, the person you marry is meant to be a permanent choice. If one partner is not committed or does not trust God with his or her life, the marriage will likely result in sorrow to both, and a painful split is much more likely. It is inviting hardship. In contrast, when the dreams of two committed people become one, it is beautiful! A man and woman with united values and purpose is the most fertile ground for love and joy, as well as for sowing seeds of goodness in the lives of those around them. All that being said and extremely important, it is also important to remember we are all human and have our shortcomings. God often brings together people who he knows will be good helpers and encouragers to each other's growth. Marriage in itself is designed to help us grow and overcome our selfish nature. While it is important to make a very prayerful and thoughtful decision about the man or woman we marry, remember we all need the grace of God and he often uses us to demonstrate that grace within the joys and challenges of married life.

Young adults, whether married or single, are involved with the exciting, yet sometimes overwhelming, activities of becoming independent. It is not easy to launch out on our own, so trusting and turning to God each step of the way is very reassuring. He can also help us to make wise decisions in how we spend our time and our finances. Will we spend it for ourselves or will we be generous and also think of others? Did you know God set a minimum amount of ten percent of our income to be given back for *his* good work? God will trust us with more as we demonstrate we are trustworthy! It is important to keep a pulse on our desires. Materialism can easily rob us of both our joy and our resources. Be on guard to keep a balance between preparing a life and home of your own and getting carried away with the vast array of things some cultures have to offer. Remember to be happy—less is more. The more things we have, the more time it takes to care for our possessions, and the less time and money we have for others. If we choose wisely, keeping a balance in our lives, we will have more freedom and contentment in the long run!

Middle age

Middle age is a time of life with added responsibility. Keeping a balance in our lives becomes especially important as we serve our families, our work, and pursue our passions. In middle age we may take a look at our lives and question our choices thus far. Every choice, good or bad, God promises to use for our ultimate good if we follow his call. "And we know that in all things God works for the good of those who love him, who have been called according to his purpose" (Romans 8:28). If we are committed to God, even when we have made bad choices, God can still use them for good. He can turn things around—our marriage, our work, our life—whatever we bring to him! We may question our choice of career or how we spend our free time. Healthy evaluation helps us to refocus our lives. What changes can we make to better align our days with our priorities. Change energizes our lives! The changing colors of the leaves and the cooler temperatures of fall, for example, can motivate us to go hiking, bake an apple pie, or curl up by the fire with someone we love. We enjoy the change of seasons, because it motives us to do new activities. Making healthy changes will give us new hope if we are weary of our routine. God may redirect us and give us a new sense of purpose, or make us aware of areas where we can improve the quality of our lives. It may be a time of recommitment to a lifelong relationship. It is a good time to renew your current relationships and initiate new ones. Encourage someone with friendship or mentor a teen that needs direction if the Spirit draws you. Middle age can be a time for God to move us in a new direction as new passions develop or God may open new opportunities in a lifelong dream. Take some time to retreat with God, time to reflect and give thanks. Seek a renewed thankfulness for the life you have been given, yet be open for a new opportunity or adventure. He has been preparing you through the good and the bad. Talk to him, listen, and expect him to guide you! It is the perfect time of life for you to use what you have learned so far to touch the lives of others.

Our Golden Years

As we enter the latter stages of life we may have a new measure of freedom and more time. If you have been blessed with retirement, use the abilities and strengths that you have acquired from a lifetime of experience to help others. There are people everywhere who can use your honed skills, expertise, and wisdom. Who in your family or neighborhood can use your encouragement and love? Be creative in seeking out people with real needs in your immediate sphere or even around the world. Nothing is more rewarding! What skills and wisdom will be lost if we do not pass them on to the next generation? Even your hobbies are something you can share. If you have grandchildren make it part of your schedule to spend time with them and talk on a regular basis. Share your life stories and teach them the skills you know. Take interest in their lives and encourage them whenever possible. Enjoy their smiles!

If our health and body decline and it becomes more difficult to get out, remember that God is still counting on us to initiate action in our world. One of the greatest and most important ways for us to do that is through prayer. Though God calls us to pray at every age, the golden years can be a special time of devotion to prayer. Pray for your family and the people in your community. Pray for our nation and our world. Pray through the news as you watch it. Pray, pray, pray! Remember, "For our struggle is not against flesh and blood, but against the rulers, against the authorities, against the powers of this dark world and against the spiritual forces of evil in the heavenly realms" (Ephesians 6:12). Having a renewed appreciation for prayer will make a great impact as we call out to God on behalf of others. Jesus intercedes in heaven and the Spirit of truth prompts us to intercede for specific people and situations on earth. Though we may not see the answers to all of our prayers until we pass into eternity, our faith will "move mountains." One day we will be gathered together to find that some of God's most powerful work on earth was accomplished through the answered prayer of his people. The Bible inspires us to pray with confidence:

> The Lord is righteous in all his ways and loving toward all he has made. The Lord is near to all who call on him, to all who call to him in truth (Psalm 145:17-18 NIV © 1985). And pray in the Spirit on all occasions with all kinds of prayers and requests. With this in mind, be alert and always keep on praying for all the Lord's people (Ephesians 6:18). He makes nations great and destroys them; he enlarges nations and disperses them (Job 12:23). "Ask the God of the harvest, therefore, to send out workers into his harvest field"

(Matthew 9:38). "In my distress I called to the Lord; I cried to my God for help. From his temple he heard my voice; my cry came before him, into his ears." (Psalm 18:6)

If we will talk with God in heartfelt prayer, we can make a difference!

"I know there is nothing better for men than to be happy and to do good while they live" (Ecclesiastes 3:12). King Solomon questioned the meaning of life and concluded that being thankfully content and caring for others is what makes life worth living! Through each stage and position in life, understanding who God is and the power he holds is the key. That is why the Bible tells us, "The fear of the Lord is the beginning of wisdom; all who follow his precepts have good understanding" (Psalm 111:10a). Knowing and trusting God, his *power* and his *love*, will help us choose and act wisely—understanding that if we disregard God we have reason to fear his judgment. For some people this is the first step. It is never, ever too late! God sees the big picture and our understanding is very limited. We will never go wrong trusting him; it is the wisest decision we can make. Jesus is the way to eternal life and future happiness! As we follow him we learn to love, becoming rich in character, and with a new found wisdom and hope we realize, "A good name is better than fine perfume, and the day of death better than the day of birth" (Ecclesiastes 7:1).

Jesus is described with the imagery of a good shepherd, one who carries his lambs on his shoulders and goes after his lost sheep (Psalm 23, Isaiah 40:11, Matthew 18:10–14, John 10:1–30). Like us, his follower Thomas wanted to know the way home (John 14:1– 5). Jesus answered, "I am the way and the truth and the life. No one comes to the Father except through me" (John 14:6). If we are willing, he will guide and sometimes even carry us home to our Father, like a shepherd who cares for his sheep. Along the journey he will lead us to places and situations where we can be fed. Jesus said that doing his Father's will was his food (John 4:32–35). He knows we are "fed" by doing God's will—"feeding" others. Our faith and character grow as we display God's love and teach his truth, serving others with our lives. Like a little hummingbird, we are fed as we spread the sweet pollen of true love so that others may experience a healthy, abundant, and eternal life. The last morning Jesus spent with his followers (on earth) he made them a fresh fish breakfast on the beach. He fed them and then knowing he was soon to ascend to heaven Jesus appealed to Peter to "feed and care for his sheep." Three times Jesus asked Simon Peter, "... do you truly love me..."... "Feed my lambs."... "...do you truly love me?" ... "Take care of my sheep." ... "Do you love me?" ... "Feed my sheep." The whole passage found in John 21 is the last story John records. Peter was hurt by Jesus repeatedly questioning his love. Yet it was for an important purpose—Peter would never forget what was most important to Jesus—the teaching and care of his people! Peter became the first teacher of the New Covenant of love, established by Jesus giving himself for us. Likewise, our own hurts can be used to help others when we turn to God. His love heals us and he uses our past to impress on us the importance of reaching out and caring for others. As we experience that God is present and active in our lives, we tell others what God has done for us, leading them to Jesus, the "bread of life" (John 6:35, 48). There is nothing more important to God! He created each man, woman, and child and he loves them all! Over and over again, he tells us if we truly love him, we need to care for others. Read Matthew 25:31-46 if you have any doubt about God's priorities; the passage is both beautiful and sobering.

Don't let life pass you by, just drifting through. Be intentional about your choices and priorities in each season of your life. Decide that your life will make a difference in the battle between good and evil that still rages on earth. Believe and act upon the promises of God. 2 Peter 3:9 tells us, "The Lord [God] is not slow in keeping his promise, as some understand slowness. Instead he is patient with you, not wanting anyone to perish, but everyone to come to repentance." God loves you and is patient. He loves all the people of the world! God invites us all to believe and work with him. He wants us to pay attention—to be aware of the people around us, learning to see them through his eyes. God enables us to overcome fear and act in true love. He has designed this brief journey of life on earth, to be an ongoing, interactive lesson of love that will ultimately bring us home. In the end, no matter what our situation, there will be nothing more important than who we have become and how we have touched the lives of others. Jesus' shed blood, his sacrifice, has made it possible for us to touch others with *true love*. We now have his presence, the Holy Spirit to help us. Don't waste this great sacrifice! Don't turn away from love; open up and embrace the gift of God's loving presence and let love pour through you to others. We can then look forward to a new life after this one, as described in the book of Revelation. "And I heard a loud voice from the throne saying, 'Look! God's dwelling place is now among the people, and he will dwell with them. They will be his people, and God himself will be with them and be their God. "He will wipe every tear from their eyes. There will be no more death" (promised in Isaiah 25:8) or mourning or crying or pain, for the old order of things has passed away.' He who was seated on the throne said, 'I am making everything new!' Then he said, 'Write this down, for these words are trustworthy and true.' He said to me: 'It is done. I am the Alpha and the Omega, the Beginning and the End. To the thirsty I will give water without cost from the spring of the water of life.'" (Revelation 21:3-6). No more death, crying, or pain, no more frustration! We cannot even fully imagine a life so beautiful, rich, and satisfying! Allow those around you to see a glimpse of this hope, this beautiful promise of what is to come, through your life. Our love can be a rainbow of hope. Set all of your heart, soul, mind, and strength on loving God and his creation. Become a part of God's family and receive your destiny— LIVING for LOVE!

Now to him who is able to do immeasurably more than
we ask or imagine, according to his power that is at work
within us, to him be glory in the church and in Jesus Christ
throughout all generations, for ever and ever! Amen.
Ephesians 3:20-21

Group Discussion:

1. What stage of life are you in? Are you content in that stage? Why or why not?
2. What were some of your best and/or worst memories in childhood? How do they affect you?
3. How might our parents' style of parenting affect how we look at ourselves, God, and/or other relationships?
4. What are you looking for in finding a person to marry? OR Why did you marry your wife or husband?
5. How has marriage and/or raising children changed you?
6. How has material wealth affected you? Have you found that more things bring you greater happiness?
7. Have you questioned decisions you have made in your life? Is there any bad decision which you are comfortable sharing, that God turned around or later used for good?
8. Are there any dreams that have been unfulfilled in your life? How has that affected you?
9. Share any hopes or dreams God has recently given to you. Are there any similar dreams within the group or ways that we could help each other?
10. As you look ahead are there any changes you would like to make?
11. As you age, what are the events or people in your life, and/or in our world, that you can have an effect on? How?
12. What is most important to you as you look back on your life?
13. What steps could you take to experience more joy and fulfillment as you go forward?

Our compassionate and creative God values relationships. He calls us to partner with him, reflecting his love and light to the world!

God gave us the wise and loving principles to live a full life, summarized in *Living for Love*. It is my hope this book has been a guide to help understand what God has revealed about his overall plan and a springboard for each of us to find our place in it. He wants us to really *see* the people around us and seek his direction as we explore ideas to reach out to others in love. This alphabetical listing of ideas, from the very simple to the elaborate, is meant to be a catalyst for God to call you to reach out in your own way, according to your interests, passions, and gifting. Please feel free to add to the list. As you read through these suggestions, don't let them overwhelm you. No one can change the world on their own. It is God's work! Each one of us takes part in a small piece of his overall plan. We need to be intentional in reflecting God's love, relying on him for the power. Pray for God to help you to discover and do the part he has planned for you!

A

Acceptance – Is there someone you know whom you could make feel included or accepted? Though important for all ages, it is especially important in the lives of students and teens.

Achievement – Write down what you would like to achieve and think about whether these goals are worthy of your time and life.

Pray for guidance as you set long-term and short-term goals to go forward.

Adventure can build relationships and open doors to learn more about God. Are you open to try something outside of your comfort zone? A new adventure can be exhilarating and give you confidence.

Afterschool Care – Start a God-based program or just help a neighbor one or more days a week.

Archeology – Much of scripture has been proven historically accurate by archeology. If this interests you, become knowledgeable and share. Perhaps you could put together a presentation for groups, such as youth or retirement homes.

Art Workshop – Invite children, teens, actually people of any age to draw and paint something that reminds them of God. Then have a time to share.

Athletics – Any sport is a great way to build relationships and integrity. Use the one you enjoy to reach out.

B

Backyard Bible Club – Invite the neighborhood children for Bible stories and crafts during a week of the summer. Child Evangelism Fellowship has great tools if coming up with your own ideas seems intimidating.

Baking – Everyone loves fresh baked breads, cakes, and cookies! It is a sweet way to break the ice with people around you.

Bible Studies – Invite people to your home for an informal Bible study and some food. You will be surprised how many will participate. (See Chapter 8)

Birthday Cards – Could you be the one who is consistent in sending a loving card to a family member, missionary, teacher, elderly, or anyone who will be touched to know you care? Share some encouraging words or news of what God has done for you lately.

Block Party or Backyard Barbeque – This is a great way to meet your neighbors and get to know them, paving the way for a meaningful relationship.

Boardwalk or City Square Outreach – Come up with a show worth watching or some riddles to solve and then follow it up by sharing your story, including a gospel presentation. Open Air Campaigners can offer training.

Boating – If you own a boat use it to bring out some young people or to entertain some neighbors you don't know well. Most things we are blessed with can also be shared to bless others.

Building Projects – Jesus' earthly father was a carpenter of good character! If you can build, and want to make an impact on young men and women, teach them. Not only will they learn a skill, but also they can learn about Jesus and loving character from your example. You could teach masonry, electrical, plumbing, roofing, or anything that you know. Better yet find someone in need and have them help you on that project. Mobile home parks are a good place to look, because the project can be small and the need great.

Bus Outreach or Just a Ride to Church – Are there children or teens in your community who have no way to get to church to enjoy the children's or youth programs? How about others who cannot drive?

C

Calling – Make that phone call that has been on your mind. Call distant friends and family to let them know you love them.

Care – Wherever you go, and whatever you do, take the time to care about the people around you! Take special care for the sick or elderly that you know or seek out someone who has no one.

Cartoons – Post cartoons that teach God's principles outside your space at work. Be sure they are encouraging.

Be sensitive about posting political satire; it may build walls rather than remove them.

Car Repair – Build a relationship with teens by helping them learn how to maintain or fix their cars. Or show you care by helping a neighbor or co-worker who is struggling financially.

Celebrations – The people who take the time to plan and prepare celebrations bring us joy. Special events, holidays, parties, and times of thanksgiving make memories. Laughter can draw us to God!

Charity – Give of your time and money for a worthy cause. A motive that is from the heart pleases God.

Charm School – Teach young girls principles from the Bible, as well as hospitality skills, grace, and manners, preparing them to be beautiful inside and out! This could be fun for a group of teens or your daughters and their friends during summer break.

Children – There are many ways to reach out to children with the love of God. Look for programs in your community for children, such as scouting or church programs, and volunteer to help. Establish a safe relationship of trust with a child who has a difficult home life. Use your imagination!

Christmas – One of the best times of year to reach out to friends, family, co-workers, students—anyone. The ideas are endless. This time of year you can give cards with a clear gospel message, you can have a dinner for neighbors, or you can throw a party at a school or retirement home. You can sing, act, cook, bake—anything God prompts you to do. It will be accepted with joy because it is Christmas! Don't be afraid to tell your story.

Church – Be sure you are part of a community of believers—followers of Jesus. Whether big or small, in a home or public building, being together is so important. Invite others as you build relationships with them.

Clinics – Creating or working in a clinic for medical or dental needs in areas where there is poverty is an amazing way to reach out. Also, creating a clinic to teach things, such as how to better care for children or budget money, is a wonderful and practical way to show the love of God.

Clothing Exchanges or Giveaways – Have a fun day with neighbors to build relationships, each bringing some clothes you no longer want. / Organize and advertise free clothes for a day (at a church or school) to reach out to the community. This may lead to further outreach as you meet people and hear about needs.

Coaching – A coach can be a model for young people—someone who demonstrates and teaches doing his or her best and relying on God. Both are essential to living a godly and joy-filled life.

Comedy – Too often comedy goes down a dark road. How refreshing it is when we hear a comedian with a clean routine that makes us laugh about life in this fallen world and points us to the God who loves us.

Communication – Is there someone in your life with whom your communication is weak or full of misunderstandings? Do your part to work on it! / Are you trained to teach communication skills to others?

Concerts – All kinds of concerts could be used for outreach. For example bring in a Christian rock band to a community venue, such as a local high school, and advertise well. Be sure and organize plenty of help.

Cooking – Teach someone to cook or provide a meal for someone who needs it. God can use you!

Crafts – Most children and women love crafts. Gather people together to do a craft and share the love of Jesus.

Cycling – An enjoyable day in the fresh air riding is a good way to build a friendship. Stop somewhere for a sandwich so you have time to talk.

D

Dance – Dance is beautiful and can be used to illustrate God's love. / Teaching dance or taking dancing lessons can both build relationships. / Organizing a dance at a church or community hall brings people together.

Defend those who cannot defend themselves!

Delight – What can you do to delight someone you care about and deepen your relationship?

Dental Care – Provide dental care to people in poverty. If you have this skill, join a mission trip for a week to help people who really need it. You will be blessed!

Dinner – Sharing food is one of the best ways to build relationships. Have people from your work or neighborhood to dinner or take them out. Bring in pizza if cost or time is an issue.

Distribution of Food – The biggest problem in feeding people in poverty is food distribution. There are many countries where unreliable government, corruption, war, or climate make this task extremely difficult. Do you have expertise in distribution? Have you ever worked in a third world country? Wouldn't it be amazing if you could help feed the hungry?

Divorced and Widowed – Reach out to those in your neighborhood who don't have spouses to come home to. Ask them to dinner once in a while; help them with their children.

Diving – My sister and brother-in-law use their hobby of scuba diving to build relationships and get away on retreat with the purpose of sharing the love of Jesus.

Dreams – Help someone to identify his or her dreams and/or help make them come true!

E

Easter is a wonderful time to plan an outreach in your community. Combine all the fun of Easter egg rolls or hunts with a clear presentation of why we celebrate Easter. Gather the children and have them participate as you ask questions and tell them why Jesus died for us, focusing on the resurrection. Let them know how much they are loved and that JESUS is ALIVE. Be sure to invite your neighbors to the Easter celebration at your church.

Easter Egg Coloring – Plan an informal day at your house to color eggs and have refreshments. Talk about the egg being a symbol of new life and that Jesus is the source of new life. This can be successful not only for children, but also for young teen age girls and the elderly.

Easter Passion Play – A drama or musical about the Easter story is a traditional Easter outreach that touches many hearts.

E-mail – Let the next e-mail you send be an encouragement to someone you know. Be sure all your communication is for a good purpose.

EMS (Emergency Medical Service) – Are you the right person to serve your community on the ambulance team? Free training is often available.

Exercise together to promote healthy living and to build relationships. Encourage each other along the way.

F

Family – Be a brother or sister, mom or dad, grandma or grandpa to someone who needs one!

Farming has potential for outreach on many levels. Teach youth how to farm and weave in the many parables about growing that Jesus taught—object lessons that instill truth. Locally you could provide crops you grow to families struggling in your community. / Beyond this, some may be called to teach farming on the mission field in a third world country.

Feed the Hungry – Make a difference by working in a food pantry, bringing a neighbor food, donating food or money and/or giving regularly to a reliable organization that distributes food in a third world country. / Those who have food readily available should give thanks and try not to take it for granted.

Fire Fighting – Many local fire companies are looking for volunteers willing to train and show up when the call for help comes. If you are in good shape this might be your way to serve and save lives.

Food Distribution – We are mentioning this again because the need is so great and it is such a difficult problem! There are many countries where unreliable government, corruption, war, and weather make this task extremely difficult. If you have expertise in distribution and/or conflict resolution, God may be able to use you!

Fishing – Depending on the boat and the catch, there is often time to talk on a fishing trip. Build friendships!

Forgiving – Reach out to those with whom you have a broken relationship. Take the first step!

Flowers – Give flowers to someone who is going through a tough time; cheer them up and build a relationship. / Give flowers anytime, for no reason at all!

Friendship – A friend loves at all times, encourages our best, and always forgives. Be a good friend to others, look for people who need a friend, and remember God is our best friend!

Fun – Having good, clean, creative fun, without sex (outside of marriage), drugs, alcohol abuse, or tearing people down is so refreshing and exhilarating for people of all ages. It is one of the best ways to build relationships.

G

Gallery – If your business has wall space, why not show some art that reflects the majesty and creativity of God. A gallery dedicated to works reflecting what God has done for humankind is also very effective in starting conversations that lead people to know Jesus. Try a creative venue, such as setting up a tent at a fair.

Games – Playing games together is fun and builds relationships—anything from a three-leg-race to charades or a board game. Have a game night. Try games where the questions help you get to know each other.

Gardening – At harvest time cut flowers or gather vegetables to give to a neighbor or shut-in. Tell them God loves them and enjoy their smile. / A community garden or garden club can build relationships.

Gas – Give a gift card for fuel to someone who struggles financially.

Get Away – Provide a weekend away for someone who needs it. You could go with them, watch their children, or just do the planning, depending on the circumstances.

Give of yourself, your time, and your money as the Spirit of truth leads you.

Government – Taking a role in community leadership has great potential for being a light in our world. Be sure to have a prayer team behind you.

Grace – Show grace when you are wronged by someone—reflect the character of God!

H

Handicapped – Include those around you who are handicapped. Find a way for them to join in the fun. / Mentor a handicapped youth or spend time to brighten their world no matter what their age.

Help – Help can be so encouraging! Help in the kitchen, in the yard, with children, wherever you are, look around and ask yourself, "How can I help here!" Helping your neighbor or coworker will win their respect!

Hiking – Going hiking with a group of friends or teens is a wonderful way to build relationships while being surrounded by the beauty of creation.

History – If you are a history buff, why not research what influence *true* followers of Jesus Christ have had on history. Give a presentation to local youth, a retirement home, or Sunday school. Do your best to make it dynamic and to include participation.

Hobbies – Turn your hobby into an avenue to build a relationship or to reach out to someone.

Holidays – Any holiday is a great reason to get people together and most have an easy bridge to acknowledge God's love for us. Many holidays *are* the celebration of what God has done for us!

Home – Provide a home to someone who needs one. Even as a temporary solution it can have a lasting impact.

Honor – Show honor to those around you and especially your parents. Plan an activity to that end.

Hospitality – Invite people to your home, even strangers in need. Enjoying a meal together or providing a place to spend the night is a wonderful way to build relationships and share our lives. Create a warm atmosphere.

Housing – Help provide affordable housing where there is a need by working on or funding a project.

Hugs – Give a hug to someone who needs it and lots to family members. Hugs are good for our health.

Human Rights – Anytime we work to bring dignity to others we are pleasing God. Fighting injustice and helping the oppressed is our duty. Is there any way you can help stop exploitation, such as human trafficking?

Humility – Having a truly humble attitude goes a long way in reflecting Jesus to others.

I

Imagination – Use your imagination to reach out to people. Get children involved, using their imaginations. We all have different strengths and the ideas are endless. Write us—we may include your idea in our next edition.

Information – Don't be afraid to give people the information that they need. Share your story—everyone needs to know God is active in our lives and he wants to guide and help us.

Insecurity – If God puts someone in your path that is unusually insecure, give this person some extra attention. Build a relationship and when the time is right let them know about the security of Jesus.

Interviews – Doing interviews with a few thought out questions at your local mall can be a great tool to take interest in people and get them thinking about God. This is fun to do as a group and you may make new friends.

Intervention – If you know of someone who is utterly destroying their lives, don't just let them do it! Try and intervene in some constructive way or find someone that can. You might not always be successful, but try.

Introduce your friends to other followers of Jesus and healthy ways to have fun.

Inspiration – Inspire someone to join you or to follow their own dreams to reach out to a world in need.

Investments – If you are good at investments, why not set aside some just for the purpose of funding outreach or missions. / Invest your time in building relationships.

Internationals – Do you work or go to school with someone from a different culture? Help them to feel more at home by inviting them to join you in some way. Learn about their culture and story. Help them with language.

J

Journey – What type of journey could you take related to outreach?

Joy – Keeping a balanced life with God at the center helps us to be joyful. Our smiles can give others confidence, so don't let weariness override your smile. Be mindful that your facial expression matches how you feel inside.

Justice – Work for justice on behalf of others!

K

Karaoke – Singing together is fun and great for building relationships. Find some songs with great lyrics about God to put in the mix.

Kindness – Brighten the world around you; take time to show kindness each day!

Kneel – Get on your knees in prayer on behalf of others. It will rock this world!

Know How – If you are especially good at something, think about how you could use your talent or skill to reach out and/or encourage someone.

L

Language – Help someone with their reading skills or to learn a new language.

Leadership – A humble, servant leader gives us vision and can lead us to accomplish mutual goals to help others. Step out and discover if you are a leader!

Learn – Taking a class is a great way to meet new people. Take a class for fun with someone you know to build a relationship or take a class that will help you with your outreach ideas. / Ask someone older to teach you something; it helps you and will make them feel appreciated.

Letters – It is a wonderful surprise to get an old fashioned letter in the mail. Does someone come to mind that would really be encouraged by a card or letter from you?

Lonely – No one should be lonely, but many are. If you are lonely, reach out to another person; ask God to show you who else might need a friend. / If you sense someone else is lonely, reach out to them!

Love – Ask God to help you do your best to show godly love to those around you. Focus on *demonstrating* your love to family and friends and soon your love will overflow to others. Ask God to help you to love your "enemy."

Lunch – Make an effort to have lunch regularly with someone who needs a friend.

M

Makeovers – A fun day of makeovers with friends can be a time to talk and build each other up. / A day with teen girls is an opportunity to talk about inner beauty.

Meals – Could you provide a meal for someone who is sick or needs help?

Media – If you are creative with media, find a positive way to use it to reach others with the good news of Jesus.

Medical Care – Doctors, nurses, technicians, anyone who is in the medical field can encourage and help heal people in need with their skills. It is a life of outreach. We are most effective when we practice the principles of true love. / All of us have opportunities to encourage and help the sick, even within our families.

Memorize – Memorize some of your favorite Bible verses and then go from there. The more you memorize the more resources you have when you talk to people about God. But that's not the only reason. It will help guide you through life, through good times and bad, like nothing else.

Memory – If you have a good memory use it to memorize peoples' names and something about them. It will go a long way to break the ice. If it's a struggle, still try to make an effort by learning some tricks of association.

Military Service – Serving in the military with the goal of honoring God, protecting, and helping the oppressed is a worthy sacrifice. Leaders in the military have a special role in guiding the young men and women under them to live for others. / Welcome home and show honor to those who serve in the military.

Missions – Reaching out to others as your number one, full time job in a culture not your own. This is living for love! The need is great, with still hundreds of people groups who have no way to hear of God's love. Millions of people have never heard the name of Jesus. If you are called, take time to prepare, stay close to God, and hang on for a challenging, but wonderful life. Even later life can be a great time to start the adventure of missions. Outreach at home prepares us. For those who are not called to another culture find your mission here at home and be mindful to help, pray for, and encourage those who are—serving as senders.

Miserable – Do you come across someone, on a regular basis, who is downright miserable? Try to bring some happiness to their lives; make it a challenge. You never know where this might lead, but be careful ☺!

Misguided – If you know someone, especially a youth, who is seriously misguided, gently and/or respectfully try to show them a better way. Take the time to build a relationship!

Mobilize – If you have an outgoing personality, be the one to mobilize people to meet a need or do an outreach project. / Share your passion for missions and pray for more workers!

Motivate – Motivate your friends and family to unplug and do something fun that includes others. / Motivate classmates or peers to reach out to the world around them. / Motivate yourself and others to explore God's word.

Music – Whether you sing, play, write, or rap, God can use your gift of music to speak to hearts. Use your talent!

N

Nanny – Caring for children is a great job for an older teen or anyone who loves kids. The love you pour into children can affect them for a life-time.

Nature – Enjoy the beach, the mountains, a lake, a river valley, a volcano or national park; wherever you go or whatever you do, the beauty of nature is a natural way to bring an appreciation of God to our minds. Bring someone with you and take in the majesty of God!

Nursing – Nurses can meet so many needs—through their jobs or through volunteering—at home or far away.

Nurture – Who does God want you to nurture toward a relationship with him?

O

Oasis – Create an oasis for someone who has been stressed out—perhaps your husband or wife.

Obey – Obeying the word of God, responding to the Spirit's guidance in our lives, demonstrates our love for God and is the path to a full and satisfied life. / Obeying our parents can lead them closer to God and also protects us.

Observe – Take a look around you, asking God to open your eyes spiritually. You may see people in a new light and discover a new way you can make a difference.

P

Parent – If you are a good parent, be a mom or dad to a youth who needs one. This can range from adoption to just having a wayward neighbor kid to dinner more often.

Pies – A home baked pie would soften anyone's heart. / How about a creative and delicious pie party?

Playtime – For children or adults play is good for the soul. From a play-group for mothers of preschool children to a neighborhood Frisbee game, initiate some fun!

Poverty – Help people in poverty in one way or another. You can give to a reputable organization, help someone you know, provide a job, or travel to serve in another country for a week, a year, or even a lifetime. Take the time to educate yourself on what really helps; it can be complicated.

Prayer is essential for all meaningful outreach. Talk to God and ask for his help and direction. Ask him to take down walls and display his love through you. Outreach targets evil and prayer is our first line of defense.

Pregnancy – Reaching out to someone who has an unexpected and/or crisis pregnancy can make all the difference. Helping one person go through a difficult pregnancy is very worthwhile and shows her God's love. / A young woman in our community started a crisis pregnancy center. There are great sources for training.

Prisons – If you know someone in prison, take time to visit and encourage them. Tell them Jesus loves them. Perhaps they are innocent; give them hope and fight for justice to set them free. / God may invite you to visit prisoners as a calling, reaching out to strangers who desperately need hope.

Problem Solving – Working together to solve a problem in your family, neighborhood, workplace, or world is a wonderful way to strengthen relationships. Team work builds bonds of love and unity.

Purity – Promote and encourage sexual purity among young people. Waiting until marriage to have sex, increases your chances for a blessed sex life in marriage. Don't be fooled by the world's contrary thinking.

Q

Quiet – Provide some quiet-time for someone who is overloaded in life.

Quilting – Gather a crafty group to work on a quilt to encourage someone, to create a memory, or to celebrate a special occasion such as a wedding. Relationships grow when we work together for a common good.

R

Racial Unity – Love and respect people of all races and religions; listen and learn from them. Fight injustice and stand up for the oppressed in a peaceful way.

Rainy Days – Put some sunshine in the life of someone who is in a "rainy day" season.

Refugees – War, poverty, and famine cause thousands of people each year to flee from their homes; show empathy! Helping refugees on an organizational level is often challenging work because of the vast need. You are giving hope on the front lines. Lead or support efforts to give haven to refugee families in your community.

Renovate – Help people to redecorate, refurbish, or remodel their space. It can cheer them up and give hope.

Respect – Show respect to those in authority, it is the first step to gaining theirs.

Show respect to yourself and all people regardless of their position. It is foundational in effective outreach!

Responsibility – Help someone you know who struggles with responsibility. Discuss steps they could take to go forward. Pray with them for God's help.

Role Model – Be a shining example by showing responsibility, kindness, contentment, and trust in God. Being open and honest when you fall short is also important. To whom are you a role model?

Runaways – Reach out to teens that run away. If you live in a city, getting involved could even save a life. Step in and protect them from harm. Show them unconditional love.

S

Sacrifice – When we are willing to sacrifice the things we want and our time for the good of others, God uses us to change lives. The joy and satisfaction often outweighs the sacrifice!

Service – How can you serve those around you? Is there a way you can use your gifts and talents or even do something you enjoy to help someone else?

Sex – Share loving sex with your husband or wife. It is "glue" for your relationship.

Short-Term Missions – A short term mission trip can be used in your own life as well as those you serve. Training and/or planning with leaders from the field you will serve will help maximize the benefits of the trip. When you arrive, focus on loving the people and be flexible!

Shut-Ins – Visit people who cannot get out, such as the elderly or sick. Just a short visit can mean so much. Bringing flowers, some music, or some special food can help break the ice.

Skills – What skill do you have that you could share with someone else?

Snow Removal – Be aware of those around you in a storm. If you are strong and have the right equipment, shoveling, snow blowing, or plowing an extra drive or walk is a gift for those who are unable, or for a single mom.

Song – Write, rap, or sing a song of love to God. Sing of his love for us. Share your song and lift our hearts!

Sponsor – Seek out a missionary to sponsor; it is hard to raise support! / How could you help sponsor someone else's dream?

Study – Study God's word with family and friends. Ask each other, "How can we put into practice what we learned today?" / Study anything that can help our world or build relationships. / Help others with a study group.

Substance Abuse – Those who are captive to drug and alcohol abuse need help from others to stop this destructive cycle. God may call you to work with an individual, start a support group, or work with addicts or alcoholics full time. / Pray for people to be set free.

Surprise – Surprises are fun! They can lift someone's spirit and show them our love.

Surfing – Perhaps you could reach out by teaching someone who has always wanted to learn.

Sympathy – Sometimes people need a sympathetic ear and someone to help them see truth. You may be the one to show them God really does care. Your understanding and love helps!

T

Talent Show – A talent show can be a fun way to bring people together and celebrate each other.

Teach – The best way to learn is to teach. Step out and discover if you have the gift of teaching. Teach what you have learned or be a leader, using a curriculum to learn together. Teach others your skills and share your life. / We can also teach about God's love and precepts by our example.

Teachers – The profession of teaching is truly a life of outreach and seems to get harder with each passing year. Support and encourage your children's teachers. Is there any practical help you could provide?

Tenderness – Affection and tenderness help people feel secure and can be shown in many appropriate ways. Feeling secure is the ground work for meaningful relationships.

Thankfulness – How can we show our appreciation to others? Expressing thanks builds and strengthens bonds.

Theatre – Plays or skits that reflect God's interaction with us in our current culture or in past history is a creative way to reach others. Build relationships as you prepare. Include people who need a supportive community.

Travel – Do you know someone who does not have anyone to take a trip with? Could you go with them?

Trouble Makers – Take time to talk with troublemakers if you are in authoriy. Ask them what they are really looking for. Help them to find it.

Trust – Be a person others can trust. Give others the chance to earn your trust. Trust God foremost!

Truth – Learn about truth, teach truth, and be truthful as you interact with others. Transparency helps others to trust you and to be receptive. / Allow the Spirit of truth to teach you to serve others in love.

Tutor – Volunteer as a tutor at the local school or to help a young person in your neighborhood.

U

Unemployed – Could you be a job creator? / Is there someone you can help to get by until they find a new job?

Unite – Are there people or groups that you could help unite for good? Be an organizer and/or peacemaker!

Urban Outreach – Cities have many difficult problems that outreach can target. Can you help bring love and hope to your city? Could your church pray and work together to solve a problem in your city!

V

Vacation – Take time to refresh by getting away with your family or friends. Consider including someone on a vacation in order to build a relationship and/or show care, appreciation, or acceptance— perhaps one of your children's friends, another family you enjoy, or even your parents. It can add to the fun. / Using vacation time for an outreach or missions trip can be very satisfying. Perhaps your family could enjoy an adventure serving together!

Valentine's Day – A great time to talk about and show God's love with cards, dinners, visits, etc.

Value yourself and the people around you. Never forget that God values and loves you beyond measure!

Violence – Fighting violence is a job for the strong of heart and mind. Perhaps this is your role. Calling on God is powerful in the difficulty of violence situations.

W

Walk with a friend that you would like to know better and encourage each other along the way—a meaningful way to get exercise.

Walls – Do your part to tear down harmful walls built by insecurity, mistrust, or hurt within your family, school, neighborhoods, or workplace.

War – Pray for war to end. Care for troops and refugees. / Do you have diplomatic skills to help bring peace?

Welcome new people in your school, neighborhood, or workplace.

Wisdom – Seek God for true wisdom and help others to do the same. Share your wisdom with love.

Work – Don't waste your time and ultimately your life. Work for good and be satisfied! Whatever your job, your work is a place where God can use you to reach others by your loving attitude and example.

Worship – Reaching out to others is one of the greatest ways you can worship God!

Y

Youth – With loving support and strong values instilled, youth is a time of wonder and idealism that can change the world. Help youth to understand truth and inspire them to love others. Reach out to young people living in difficult family situations. Foster and support their dreams and encourage them to use their talents for good.

Z

Zeal – Receiving God's love and showing true love to others, will give you a zeal that sparkles!

Acknowledgements

Thank you to my lovely and wise daughter Katie, the first and one of the last, to edit *Living for Love.* Her early suggestions were what made the book take shape. Katie's knowledge of grammar was valuable and her insight influenced the final touches. My wonderful sister Nancy also provided helpful input and hope from beginning to end. Her kind encouragement helped me to have the strength to continue working and not give up! I am eternally grateful. Thank you to Joshua who helped me with structure and to keep the message real. Thank you to all of my friends who were willing to help with editing and also encouraged me along the way: Faith, Hedy, Shelia, Cristina, Jen, and Betty. Soon after *Living for Love* was submitted I started treatment for stage four neck cancer. WestBow's editorial review suggested an additional edit to meet current standards in Christian publishing and smooth out some formatting. I am very grateful to my talented Aunt Sue who helped with a final edit that addressed their concerns and suggestions. When I was too weak to carry on, though we live on opposite ends of the country, God called her to help and encourage me. I also want to acknowledge my innovative son Jeffree, who makes the most of each day and my sweet daughter Sarah, whose loving nature and perseverance is admirable. Last, I would like to thank my husband Alan who allows me the freedom to follow God's call. I love and appreciate each of you!

Bibliography

Books:

Batterson, Mark. (2011). *The Circle Maker: Praying Circles Around Your Biggest Dreams and Greatest Fears.* Grand Rapids: Zondervan.

Burman, Gracia. (2003). *In the Presence of My Enemies.* Wheaton: Tyndale House.

Stanley, Andy. (2009). Starting Point: Find Your Place in the Story, (A Spiral Bound Study Guide). Grand Rapids: Zondervan.

Tucker, Ruth Ann. (1983). *From Jerusalem to Irian Jaya,* Grand Rapids: Zondervan.

Holy Bible:

Common English Bible (CEB). (2011) Nashville: Common English Bible.

New International Version (NIV). (2011) Grand Rapids: Zondervan.

New International Version (NIV). (1985) Grand Rapids: Zondervan.

New Living Translation (NLT). (2007) Illinois: Tyndale House.

Film:

Johnson, B., Kosove, A., Netter, G. (Producers), & Hancock, J. (Director). (2009). *The Blind Side*. United States: Warner Brothers Pictures.

Online Dictionaries:

merriam-webster.com
urbandictionary.com

Websites:

Feldman, Robert S. (2002) How often does the average person lie? Journal of Basic and Applied Psychology. Retrieved Dec. 4, 2012 from http://Curiosity.discovery.com (This website can no longer be found.) Retrieved June 8, 2016 from https://www.umass.edu/newsoffice/article/umass-amherst-researcher -finds-most-people-lie-everyday-conversation

Williams, Dr. Lisa. (2014) Why you should always say 'thank you': It's not just good manners – the two words helps [sic] maintain relationships, study claims. *Daily Mail, Science,* Article-2747790, Retrieved Oct., 2015 from http://www.dailymail.co.uk/sciencetech/article-2747790/Why-say-thank-It-s-not-just-good-manners-two-words-help-maintain-relationships-study-claims.html

Cru (2016) cru.org/how-to-know-god/would-you-like-to-know-god-personally

About the Author

Elise Froelicher Olson earned a Bachelor of Arts Degree in 2005 from Washington Bible College, where she also received the Christian Service Award. After suggesting to her children that a year of biblical study would be valuable, she decided to take the advice herself and continued on to earn her degree. Elise also has an Associate in Applied Science Degree for Mechanical Design and worked in the design field in her early adult years. Soon raising her three children became her purpose and she was blessed to be a stay-at-home parent. During the children's teen years Elise owned and managed Pedal Stop Ice Cream Shop in northern Virginia, in which all profits supported world missions. The whole family and many neighborhood teens, as well as the homemade ice cream, make Pedal Stop a place that was loved by its customers. Elise has volunteered with youth and missions throughout her adult life and currently enjoys working with international students at home and around the world.

Printed in the United States
By Bookmasters